Visions and Dreams

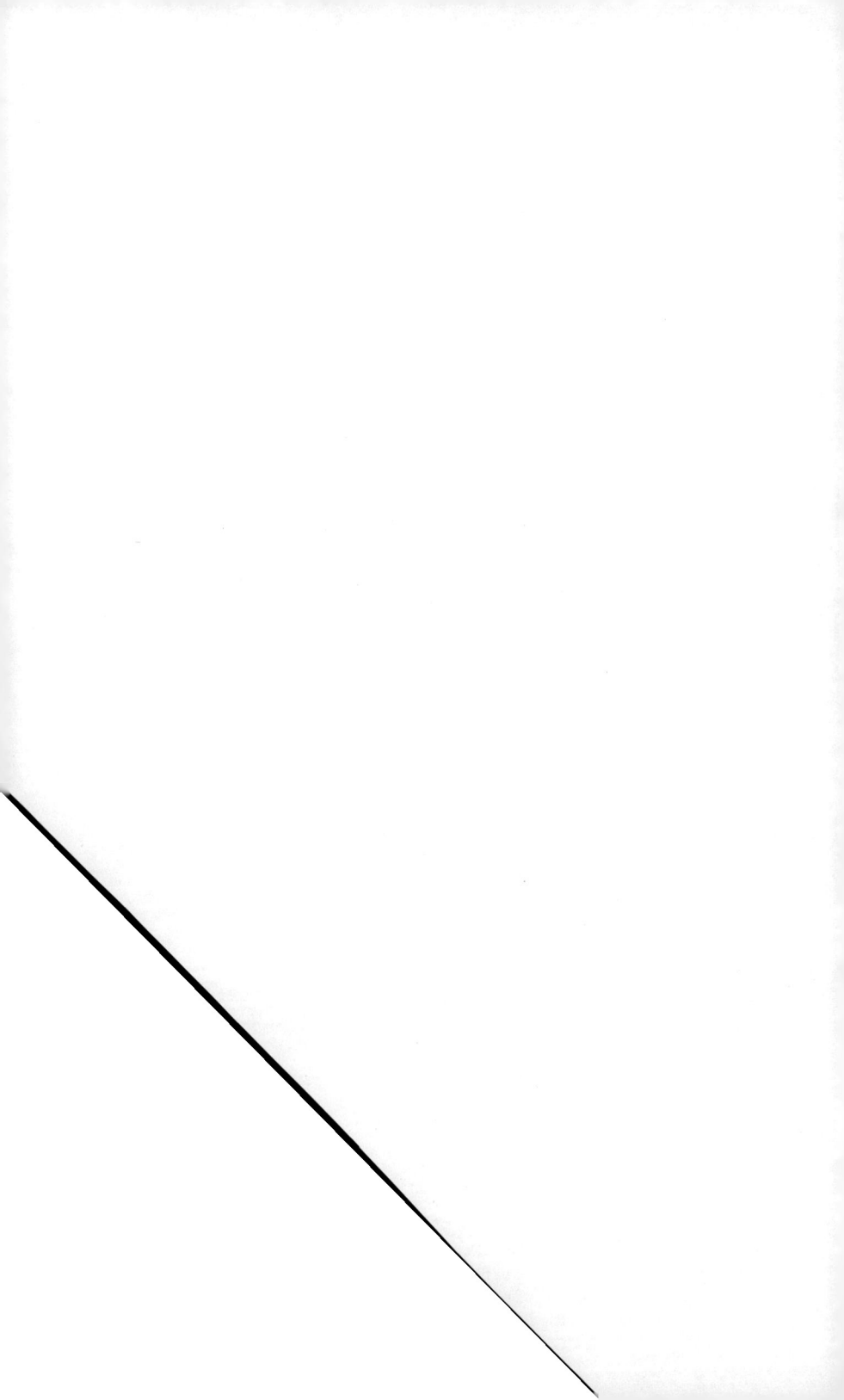

VISIONS AND DREAMS

Prophetic Gifts of the Holy Spirit

DANA GEORGE COTTRELL

Copyright © 2011 Dana George Cottrell

All rights reserved. No part of this book may be used or reproduced by any means, graphic, electronic, or mechanical, including photocopying, recording, taping or by any information storage retrieval system without the written permission of the publisher except in the case of brief quotations embodied in critical articles and reviews.

WestBow Press books may be ordered through booksellers or by contacting:

WestBow Press
A Division of Thomas Nelson
1663 Liberty Drive
Bloomington, IN 47403
www.westbowpress.com
1-(866) 928-1240

Because of the dynamic nature of the Internet, any web addresses or links contained in this book may have changed since publication and may no longer be valid. The views expressed in this work are solely those of the author and do not necessarily reflect the views of the publisher, and the publisher hereby disclaims any responsibility for them.

Certain stock imagery © Thinkstock.
Any people depicted in stock imagery provided by Thinkstock are models, and such images are being used for illustrative purposes only.

Scripture quotations are from the New King James Version.
Copyright 1979, 1980, 1982, Thomas Nelson Inc., Publishers

ISBN: 978-1-4497-2147-3 (e)
ISBN: 978-1-4497-2148-0 (sc)
ISBN: 978-1-4497-2149-7(hc)

Library of Congress Control Number: 2011912203

Printed in the United States of America

WestBow Press rev. date: 7/27/2011

www.danacottrell.net
danacottrell@sbcglobal.net

Dedication: To my grandchildren: Tyler, Luke, Shayla, Jadyn, Nathaniel, and Andrew and
To my Saturday morning prayer partners at Faith Chapel, Spring Valley, CA

Many thanks to: Pastors Graham and Pamela Truscott for their excellent teaching ministry and to Pastor Larry Pierce for reviewing my book

Contents

Preface ix
Introduction xvii
Chapter 1. Visions 1
Chapter 2. Dreams... 13
Chapter 3. The Purpose of a Prophet............................. 18
Chapter 4. Cults 22
Chapter 5. Knowledge, Understanding, and Wisdom 25
Chapter 6. Training.. 33
Chapter 7. Prayer... 50
Chapter 8. A Message to God's People 56
Chapter 9. Proverbs... 68
Chapter 10. Prophecies to Individuals 75
Chapter 11. To Church Leaders....................................... 94
Chapter 12. Warnings to the Nation 107
Chapter 13. Spiritual Warfare and Deliverance.............119
Chapter 14. Seeing into the Future................................ 126
Chapter 15. Prophecies Involving Personal Events....... 133
Chapter 16. End-Time Prophecies.................................145
Chapter 17. Nutrition.. 158
Chapter 18. Conclusion... 163

Preface

Where are we today in the circle of Christianity? In its early stages, the Christian church focused on ministering the Word of God and prayer. Doctrinal truths, the outpouring of the Holy Spirit, and signs and wonders were part of the faith, as evidenced through divine healings. Under Roman rule, Christianity suffered great persecution until it was adopted as a state religion. During this time, subtle and gradual changes took place as the church compromised with worldly influences. Following the fall of Rome, the imperial church transitioned to what became known as a medieval church. At this point, doctrinal truths were hidden, and the bulk of Christianity languished for a thousand years in a period known as the Dark Ages.

However, with the advent of reformers like Martin Luther, John Calvin, and John Knox, the light began to shine anew. Truth began to be restored as Christianity began to circle back toward the power of the early church. Martin Luther restored the doctrine of justification by faith. The Anabaptists restored the truth of baptism by full immersion. Men of God began to preach that there was more to the Christian experience than doctrinal correctness. John Wesley preached that those in Christ are new creatures, and as such, they have the responsibility to live as new creatures. This preaching became part of the holiness movement of the eighteenth and nineteenth centuries. During the twentieth century, we saw the advent of revivals involving speaking in tongues and the gift of healing, a period some refer to as the Pentecostal Movement.

Have we come full circle to the strength of the early church in terms of truth, signs, and wonders? Has truth been fully restored? Joel makes the following statement:

> And it shall come to pass afterward that *I will pour out My Spirit on all flesh; your sons and your daughters shall prophesy, your old men shall dream dreams, your young men shall see visions* (Joel 2:28).

Are old men dreaming dreams and young men seeing visions? Is the latter rain greater than the former rain? Is the Holy Spirit being poured out on our sons and daughters? If not, perhaps Christianity needs a little more time to complete the circle.

It is generally understood that the message of the cross is the gift of salvation through Jesus Christ. At the time of His return, the Lord wants a great harvest. To accomplish this goal, the gospel of the kingdom must be preached throughout the world.

> And this gospel of the kingdom will be preached in all the world as a witness to all the nations, and then the end will come (Matt. 24:14).

The signs of the times indicate that we are nearing the return of our Savior and Lord. Reformation and holiness movements not only promote evangelism but also appear to be steps toward developing within believers the mind and will of God. If this is the end game, then what is the next step? The answer may be found in Joel.

> And also on My menservants and on My maidservants I will pour out My Spirit in those days. And I will show wonders in the heavens and in the earth: Blood and fire and pillars of smoke. The sun shall be turned into darkness, and the moon into blood, before the coming of the great and awesome day of the Lord. And it shall come to pass that whoever calls on the name of the Lord shall be saved. For in Mount Zion and in Jerusalem there shall be deliverance, as the Lord has said, among the remnant whom the Lord calls (Joel 2:29–32).

The gift of visions and dreams appears to be one of the final steps to encourage people to decide to follow Christ and develop within themselves the mind and will of God. The Lord made reference to visions and dreams when He spoke to Moses.

> Suddenly the Lord said to Moses, Aaron, and Miriam, "Come out, you three, to the tabernacle of meeting!" So the three came out. Then the Lord came down in the pillar of cloud and stood in the door of the tabernacle, and called Aaron and Miriam. And they both went forward. Then He said, "Hear now My words: *If there is a prophet among you, I, the Lord, make Myself known to him in a vision; I speak to him in a dream. Not so with My servant Moses; he is faithful in all My house. I speak with him face to face, even plainly, and not in dark sayings;* and he sees the form of the Lord …" (Num. 12:4–8).

A dark saying is hidden communication where the meaning must be discovered, unraveled, or understood. These sayings can be very simple or very complex. To understand what has been said, the receiver must meditate on it and allow the Holy Spirit to reveal its meaning.

> Hear this, all you peoples; Give ear, all you inhabitants of the world, both low and high, rich and poor together. My mouth shall speak wisdom, and the meditation of my heart shall bring understanding. I will incline my ear to a proverb; I will disclose my dark saying on the harp (Ps. 49:1–4).

Basically, the psalmist hears a proverb, interprets it, and then applies its meaning in the form of a psalm. A proverb is knowledge of a dark saying. Meditating on the proverb and interpreting its meaning leads to understanding. Applying what has been revealed is wisdom. Jesus often spoke in figurative language.

> All these things Jesus spoke to the multitude in parables; and without a parable He did not speak to them (Matt. 13:34).

> These things I have spoken to you in figurative language; but the time is coming when I will no longer speak to you in figurative language, but I will tell you plainly about the Father (John 16:25).

A vision is something seen in the mind while awake. It's like a supernatural appearance in the spiritual realm. It consists of objects that are symbols and types of a hidden saying. It falls into the category of dark sayings that are hidden messages that must be interpreted to discover their meaning. They differ from dreams in that a dream consists of images passing through the mind during sleep.

The world is approaching the latter days, a time when the Lord will pour out His Spirit. At this time, a diverse range of gifts will be handed out for the building up of the church.

> Pursue love, and desire spiritual gifts, but especially that you may prophesy ... Even so you, since you are zealous for spiritual gifts, let it be for the edification of the church that you seek to excel (1 Cor. 14:1, 12).

The church will be edified by the Spirit of counsel, power, and truth in the form of knowledge, understanding and wisdom.

> And I will pray the Father, and He will give you another Helper, that He may abide with you forever the Spirit of truth, whom the world cannot receive, because it neither sees Him nor knows Him; but you know Him, for He dwells with you and will be in you (John 14:16, 17).

> However, when He, the Spirit of truth, has come, He will guide you into all truth; for He will not speak on His own authority, but whatever He hears He will speak; and He will tell you things to come (John 16:13).

The Holy Spirit of truth will work through various ministries to build up the church.

> And He Himself gave some to be apostles, some prophets, some evangelists, and some pastors and teachers, for the equipping of the saints for the work of ministry, for the edifying of the body of Christ, (Eph. 4:11, 12)

Two way communication gives the Lord an opportunity to demonstrate His love by helping His people get through troubling issues or troubled times. The Lord is the Prince of Peace. Through visions and dreams, the Lord is able to lift people up and bring comfort and peace in their lives. Individuals, as well as churches, are like sailing ships on the sea. Hearing from the Lord by way of the Holy Spirit provides wind for the sails and a hand on the rudder to give us direction.

Acquiring the gift of prophetic visions and dreams will raise a person's level of Christianity to one of unshakeable faith. In general, Christian churches recognize pastors, teachers, and evangelists. However, most shy away from prophesies and apostleship, believing that the apostolic ministry died in its infancy.

Be that as it may, as reiterated in Acts 2:17-21, Joel 2:28–29 will be fulfilled. Some of the brethren will dream dreams and see visions. To receive such gifts would be an honor. To be able to interpret them is another thing. Who among the servants of the Lord are schooled or skilled in the art of interpretation?

Is there a place where visionaries can go to learn this art? Is there a school where instructors are trained in the art of interpreting the signs of the times, dreams, and visions? When one receives a communication from God, many questions arise. First, is the communication actually from God? It could very well be of demonic origin. Second, if it is from God, what is the interpretation? Third, who is the object of the communication?

Is it for the receiver? Is it for someone else? Is it for a group of people? Or is it for all mankind to hear?

The receivers, called prophets, have responsibilities when handling these gifts. What if the gifts are misused? What if the wrong interpretation is given? What if the prophecy results in a wrong decision that harms a person in some way, shape, or form?

There were many prophets in the Old Testament. A number of them associated with each other. Undoubtedly, they shared their prophecies with one another and perhaps assisted each other in interpreting the words of the Lord, whether they were words placed in the mind or came in the form of a dream or vision.

> A wise man will hear and increase learning, and a man of understanding will attain wise counsel, to understand a proverb and an enigma, the words of the wise and their riddles (Prov. 1:5–6),

Training is an essential requirement for a prophet to quickly mature in the gifts of prophetic dreams and visions. Training can be provided from a school of prophets or simply by working with someone who has experience with the prophetic. The primary teacher is the Holy Spirit.

There are few rules for interpreting dreams and visions. To have a fixed set of rules would place the Lord in a box and restrict the methods by which the Lord may communicate information or answers to questions. For example, a person may ask the Lord a question and expect the answer in the form of a vision. The Lord may instead place a song on that person's heart, and the words of the song may be the answer to the question. Reception and interpretation require an open mind.

The main rule to follow is that any interpretation must not contradict the holy Scriptures. If a spiritual gift is misused, the gift will be taken away. For example, God freely gives visions. They should be freely and appropriately shared with others. To sell the gift for profit or to use it to deceivingly manipulate people or situations will result in the gift being removed.

The author wrote this book to share his experiences with other visionaries and with those who have a general interest in the topic of visions and dreams. Receiving, interpreting, and sharing these communications is a maturing process. Without a source to assist someone who just received the gift, the process of interpreting visions and dreams can be quite a struggle.

Introduction

In the mid-eighties, while attending a charismatic, nondenominational church, the Spirit of the Lord seemed to be weighing on my heart and mind in a powerful way. I had made a decision to follow Jesus quite some time earlier, but now was the right time to be baptized. In addition to the water baptism, I wanted the pastor to lay hands on me for the infilling of the Holy Spirit. My pastor, Dr. Graham Truscott, mentioned that when he was baptized, he felt a strong wind blow upon him. During the laying on of hands, I was hoping or perhaps expecting a mighty wind to blow upon me as evidence of the infilling. To my disappointment, I felt nothing.

About two weeks later, I had just laid down for the evening when I immediately saw a vision of a man's head. The colors in the vision were white and brown, as if I were looking at an aged black-and-white picture. I realized that this must have been a vision and wondered if I was given the gift of visions by the laying on of hands during my baptism.

Within a short time, I began to have prophetic dreams. After this, I began to feel the presence of the Holy Spirit on numerous occasions, especially during worship services and group prayer meetings. It was at group prayer meetings where I experienced countless visions, most of which I wrote down.

I felt the strongest presence of the Holy Spirit while attending a Jimmy Swaggart gathering at the Sports Arena in San Diego, California. I was standing in the background while those who went forward repeated the invitational prayer. As I was saying it along with them, a strange feeling began at my feet and filled my whole body. It was so powerful that I wanted to shout and jump for joy. However, I had just come out of a Baptist background and had not yet acclimated to the charismatic mindset, and my reserved, conservative Christian state held me back. Incidentally, one of my sons went forward to accept the Lord that evening.

When I was five or six years old, my dad returned one night from a Pentecostal Sunday evening church service. Apparently, he had been overcome by the Spirit and began dancing in the Spirit in church. He was so filled with the Spirit that when he returned home, he wanted to continue dancing. I later asked him what it was like to be filled with the Spirit. He told me, "When you are filled with the Spirit, you will know it." My question was answered at the Jimmy Swaggart meeting.

Receiving the gift of visions from the Lord was very exciting. It was like breaking through a barrier in the spirit world. I was very cautious, as I had a number of concerns related to the visions. I questioned whether they were from the Lord or from a demonic source and whether my interpretations of them were correct. I discussed this with several pastors. Since they did not have my particular gift, they could not answer my questions. When presented with my visions, their basic response was, "Thanks for being sensitive to the Holy Spirit." My small group coach and one of my Sunday school teachers did take an interest in the visions.

Sometime during 1992 I received an audible word from the Lord. By audible, I mean that it's like hearing with the mind's ear as opposed to seeing with the mind's eye, as happens in visions. The audible word was strong and was not associated with a vision.

There are times when I am seeing visions that I will ask the Lord what a particular symbol meant, and the Spirit will respond with what I would call a softly spoken answer (on the order of a thought).

I heard the audible voice on a Sunday night. I had decided to stay home from church. My wife and sons went without me. As I sat down at my desk, I began reading the Bible. (It was during a time when I was reading through the whole Bible.) I came across a passage in Luke that drew my attention. Puzzled by what I read, I asked a question, either to myself or to the Lord (I can't remember which) about the meaning of the passage. After finishing the chapter, I decided it was time to make a sandwich and headed toward the kitchen. For some reason, I felt a drive to go outside by the pool and praise God. I did so in tongues. It was a very short praise session. When I entered the house and again headed toward the kitchen, my mind heard two Greek words. The words were strong enough that I stopped in my tracks and asked the question, "Why those two words?" Then I realized that they were the answer to the question I had asked while reading the Bible.

For a brief moment, perhaps seconds, it seemed like a fire hose of information was flowing into me, and I began to ponder and understand various Scriptures. Then it dawned on me that not only did the Lord answer the question, but the Lord actually spoke to me. Needless to say, I broke out with extreme excitement. Being a rather reserved individual, I was glad my wife and kids were at church so they could not see me prance about the living room shouting. In a roundabout way, these two words led to my thesis topic for obtaining my master's degree in biblical studies and eventually to my latest book, *Genesis 1—The Design and Plan for the Kingdom of Heaven*.

As mentioned earlier, the prophet Joel stated that in the latter days, the Lord will pour out His Spirit, and young men will see visions and old men will dream dreams. I must be somewhere in between young and old, as I have experienced both.

Without a school of prophets, those who receive the gift of visions or prophetic dreams will find it difficult to deal with and handle the gifts. It takes time to mature in the handling of these gifts. This book was written not to expound on the author but to provide a guide to future prophets for them to mature in handling the gifts.

I will present many examples of visions and dreams I have received over a twenty-two-year period. It is my hope that as I share my experiences, others can avoid the pitfalls of moving too quickly in the gift, of misinterpretation, of knowing when to act and not to act on a prophecy, of operating outside of a spiritual covering, of not writing down the prophecy, of misdirecting a prophecy, or of not taking the time to hear the word of the Lord.

Notes:

(1) The nondenominational charismatic church I attended in the eighties was originally named Restoration Temple. It later became Mission Bay Christian Fellowship (MBCF). The name has again changed. MBCF is used when referencing this church.

(2) As a general rule during group prayer sessions, the names of people and their associated issues are kept confidential within the group. This rule is enforced in order to avoid uneasiness and embarrassing situations relative to those who are being prayed for. Therefore, the names of individuals associated with visions received during the prayer meetings are not mentioned.

CHAPTER 1

Visions

Introduction

A vision is something seen in the mind while awake. It's like a supernatural appearance in the spiritual realm. It consists of dark sayings, which are hidden messages that must be interpreted to discover the meaning. They differ from dreams in that a dream consists of images passing through the mind during sleep. From my experience, visions seem to fall into two categories. One category consists of fixed objects that are symbols and types of a hidden saying. The other category consists of images in motion, such as someone riding a horse.

Some images are in black and white. Others are in vivid colors. The images are in focus, clear, and crisp. When the visions appear, I feel like I'm in a hypnotic trance. There can be praying or harmonious singing or music in the background and I will not be distracted. However, sharp noises or distractions, such as a baby crying, a ringing telephone, a loud voice, children running about, or a clanging cymbal, will distract me from the vision. I have had visions broken up by such distractions in one Sunday service only to have them completed during another service.

Most visions occur during prayer sessions. Some occur while I am awakening from sleep. Others occur during worship or during simple meditation during my own quiet time.

Occasionally I will question the meaning of something seen with my mind's eye, and I will hear an answer with my mind's ear (like an inserted thought, if you will).

I write most of my visions down. I title and date them. I generally describe the background. For example, if the theme of a prayer session during which I see a vision is on church growth, this is important, as it may help to interpret the vision. If I ask a question, the background is the asking of a question. However, the vision may not relate to any particular issue going on in the background. The Lord may simply want to get a point across.

It's important to write down the details of the vision as soon as possible. The longer one waits, the more that is forgotten. However, having been guilty of waiting too long, the Lord sometimes reminds me of a detail left out of a vision.

The interpretation may not come quickly. Some visions may be quite simple to interpret. For example, while praying in a small group, I once saw a vision of a mug of beer with a pair of scissors underneath of it. The obvious interpretation was "cut out drinking beer." Someone in the group had issues that were the result of a drinking problem. Most visions can be interpreted in short order. Others simply need to be put on the back burner for a while. I've interpreted some of these months later.

Interpretation is subject to the prophet. The Lord knows the mind of the prophet. He knows a person's experiences and education level, and He may draw from these experiences to get a point across. As no two snowflakes are alike, no two people have the same experiences.

Visions in the Old Testament

As mentioned earlier, the Lord spoke to Moses directly. However, to others He spoke in dark sayings.

> Then He said, "Hear now My words: *If there is a prophet among you, I, the Lord, make Myself known to him in a vision; I speak to him in a dream. Not so with My servant Moses; he is faithful in all My house. I speak with him face to face, even plainly, and not in dark sayings;* and he sees the form of the Lord ..." (Num. 12:6–8).

The Lord spoke to the major and minor prophets in visions. For example, the Lord used the method of visions to speak to Isaiah.

> The *vision* of Isaiah the son of Amoz, *which he saw* concerning Judah and Jerusalem in the days of Uzziah, Jotham, Ahaz, and Hezekiah, kings of Judah (Isa. 1:1).

> The *word that Isaiah* the son of Amoz *saw* concerning Judah and Jerusalem (Isa. 2:1).

The method by which the word of the Lord came to Jeremiah is uncertain. Jeremiah did not appear to receive his information by way of visions. When he prophesies, it appears that the Lord is speaking through him.

> Then the word of the Lord came to me [Jeremiah], saying: "Before I formed you in the womb I knew you; before you were born I sanctified you; I

> ordained you a prophet to the nations ..." (Jer. 1:4–5).

> Then the Lord put forth His hand and touched my mouth, and the Lord said to me: "Behold, I have put My words in your mouth" (Jer. 1:9).

The Lord spoke to Jeremiah but not face to face as He did with Moses. Ezekiel saw visions and heard from the Lord, but there is no evidence that it was a face-to-face contact.

Daniel saw many visions and had great skill in interpreting the visions as well as dreams.

> As for these four young men, God gave them knowledge and skill in all literature and wisdom; and Daniel had *understanding in all visions and dreams* (Dan. 1:17).

Of the minor prophets, Zechariah seemed to be the most outspoken visionary. He had a vision of horses, horns, the measuring line, the high priest, the lampstand and olive trees, the flying scroll, the woman in a basket, and the four chariots. The following are examples of how some of the other minor prophets received the word of the Lord:

> The *words* of Amos, who was among the sheepbreeders of Tekoa, *which he saw* concerning Israel ... (Amos 1:1).

> The *vision of Obadiah*. Thus says the Lord God ... (Obad. 1:1).

> The *word of the Lord* that came to Micah of Moresheth in the days of Jotham, Ahaz, and Hezekiah, kings of Judah, *which he saw* concerning Samaria and Jerusalem (Mic. 1:1).
>
> The burden against Nineveh. The book of the *vision of Nahum* the Elkoshite (Nah. 1:1).
>
> The burden *which the prophet Habakkuk saw* (Hab. 1:1).

The prophecies of both the major and minor prophets are so well written that it is difficult to believe that everything written came from interpreting visions. However, most certainly the Holy Spirit is sufficient enough to make this happen. I suspect that for the most part, the Spirit entered the prophets, and they spoke or recorded as the Spirit gave utterance. This is hinted at in Ezekiel when the Spirit entered him while the Lord was speaking to him.

> Then the Spirit entered me when He spoke to me, and set me on my feet; and I heard Him who spoke to me (Ezek. 2:2).

As mentioned earlier, the Lord touched the mouth of Jeremiah and said that He would speak through him. I have heard people in the congregation speak the words of the Lord. I certainly lack that gift. However, I seem to have a gift of discernment and have found that when asking the Lord whether the words are from Him, the Spirit will move within me. When I feel the Spirit, I'm generally certain that it is the Lord speaking through an individual. I have heard people speak in tongues, followed by someone who interprets the tongues.

It is difficult for a visionary to speak out during the appropriate time in a church service, as it takes time to interpret the vision. Also, I find it best to provide the vision and its interpretation to the pastor (or a pastor) of the church for approval. That way, I don't risk usurping the authority of the church.

The following are example interpretations from three of my visions:

> I am coming to gather My bride. Be prepared as the wise virgins. Keep your lamps full. Do not be as the foolish virgins who run off to have their lamps filled when I come. I am calling My bride to enter the land of milk and honey and drink My sweet wine.
>
> I am He who moves upon the face of the waters. I am the light of the world. I am impressing upon you to read the Word of God and let my Spirit flow through you.
>
> Listen to what the Spirit has to say. The nation has become offensive to My sight. They have drunk from the cup of fornication. It is a great nation. I shall bring calamity upon it. There shall be wailing and gnashing of teeth. Beware of the beast.

If a visionary speaks out during a church service, the church leader is put in a position to either receive or not receive the spoken word. The first two interpretations above may be acceptable to the church leader. However, he or she may not agree with the third one. Not receiving the spoken word puts the church leader in an awkward position with the visionary, as well as the congregation. Therefore, it's best to share the vision with the leader at a more convenient time.

The Tabernacle of Moses
The tabernacle of Moses depicted a shadow of things to come. It was a type of the kingdom of heaven, the body of Christ.

> Jesus answered and said to them, "Destroy this temple, and in three days I will raise it up … But He was speaking of His body (John 2:19, 21).

The tabernacle of Moses was divided into three sections: the outer court, the inner court or Holy Place, and the Holy of Holies. Entrance to the tabernacle represents Jesus or the one way by which we may enter into the kingdom of heaven.

> I am the door. If anyone enters by Me, he will be saved … (John 10:9).

There were two items in the outer court: the brazen altar and the brazen laver. The brazen altar in the outer court points to the ultimate sacrifice of Jesus Christ. Priests used the brazen laver to wash their hands and feet before entering the inner court. Thus the laver represents cleansing ourselves in the Word of God daily.

> That He might sanctify and cleanse it with the washing of water by the word (Eph. 5:26).

Moving inward within the tabernacle, there were three primary items in the inner court: the table of showbread, the golden candlestick, and the altar of incense. The golden candlestick had seven lamps and was the only light in the inner court. Although much could be said about this artifact, basically the lampstand represents Jesus as the light of the world. The seven lamps represent the sevenfold Spirit.

> And there were seven lamps of fire burning before the throne, which are the seven Spirits of God (Rev. 4:5).

The sevenfold Spirit is described in Isaiah 11:

> There shall come forth a Rod from the stem of Jesse, and a Branch shall grow out of his roots. The Spirit of the Lord shall rest upon Him, the Spirit of wisdom and understanding, the Spirit of counsel and might, the Spirit of knowledge and of the fear of the Lord ... But with righteousness He shall judge the poor (Isa. 11:1–4).

The twelve loaves of bread upon the table of showbread represent the spiritual food of the apostolic ministry. Jesus is the bread of life. Since we are a part of the body of Christ, we are the bread of life.

> For we being many, are one bread and one body; for we all partake of that one bread (1 Cor. 10:17).

The wine at the table represents the blood that was shed for our sins.

> Whoever eats My flesh and drinks My blood has eternal life ... (John 6:54).

The altar of incense speaks of what we have to offer up to the Lord. At this altar we offer up prayer, praise, intercession, and worship. When people lift up their hands before the Lord in praise during worship, can they look back over the past week, examine their actions, and feel comfortable in offering their choices as a sweet fragrance to the Lord?

In Leviticus God defined for Moses the type of incense to be burned at this altar. Any other incense was unacceptable. In the same way, God desires only offerings from us that honor Him.

> Then Nadab and Abihu, the sons of Aaron, each took his censer and put fire in it, put incense on it, and offered profane fire before the Lord, which He had not commanded them. So fire went out from the Lord and devoured them, and they died before the Lord. Then Moses said to Aaron, "This is what the Lord spoke, saying: 'By those who come near Me I must be regarded as holy; And before all the people I must be glorified ...'" (Lev. 10: 1–3).

Last, within the Holy of Holies was a relic that many have sought after—the ark of the covenant. The ark was a large, ornate box decorated with two angels (cherubim) perched on each end with a golden mercy seat between them. The ark had a chest that contained manna, Aaron's rod that budded, and the tablets of the law. Manna is a foreshadowing of Jesus, who is the bread of life. Aaron's rod that budded suggests life after death. The tablets of the law lead us to Christ. The mercy seat on the ark implies the righteous judgment of Christ. The two cherubim represent knowledge and understanding of the ways of God. It is here where the Lord will speak between the wings of the cherubim.

> And there I will meet with you, and I will speak with you from above the mercy seat, from between the two cherubim … (Ex. 25:22).

Christians have access to the Holy of Holies because Jesus is our high priest and the high priest had direct access to the Holy of Holies. This position of Christ as High Priest was signified when the veil that hid the Holy of Holies from the public was torn in two from top to bottom at the time of the crucifixion. With this great final act, the Lord wants us to dwell in the Holy of Holies. However, some insist on staying in the outer court. Others will go no further than the Holy Place. Blessed are those who go all the way to the Holy of Holies.

In general, to receive visions and dreams from the Lord, one must enter the Holy of Holies. It is here that the Lord speaks between the wings of the cherubim. If a visionary is walking through a wilderness or a dry place (prophetic visions and dreams have ceased or minimized), then he or she must check the incense being offered to the Lord (i.e., the way of his or her life).

Bear in mind that dwelling in the Holy of Holies does not require a state of perfection. It requires the right heart attitude toward God and a persevering mindset to develop within oneself the mind of Christ.

The Tabernacle of David
Following a battle in which the Philistines defeated Israel, the Philistines captured the ark of the covenant. In preparation of the

recovery and return of the ark, David pitched a tent for it in what was named the city of David or Zion. Zion was a place within the city of Jerusalem. Upon its return, the ark was placed in the tent, and it was there that David celebrated before the Lord with dance, food, and music. (See 1 Chronicles 10–16.) The tent and the ark within are referred to as the Tabernacle of David. All this was taking place while regular worship was going on in the tabernacle of the Lord at Gibeon.

Today, as a result of the veil being torn following the crucifixion of Jesus Christ, we have access to the Holy of Holies, which contains the spiritual ark of the covenant. There we can dance and worship before the Lord our God as David did before the physical ark in Zion. The tabernacle of David is being restored.

There are two references to the tabernacle of David.

> On that day I will raise up the tabernacle of David, which has fallen down, and repair its damages; I will raise up it ruins, and rebuild it as in the days of old (Amos 9:11).

> After this I will return and will rebuild the tabernacle of David which has fallen down. I will rebuild its ruins, and I will set it up, so that the rest of mankind may seek the Lord, even all the Gentiles who are called by My name, says the Lord who does all these things (Acts 15:16–17).

These verses speak of the restoration of the church and the building up of a glorious habitation for the Spirit of God to bring a harvest of souls to Christ.

Conclusion

So, who is able and willing to enter the Holy of Holies and receive prophetic visions and dreams? None of us are perfect, but those who persevere and strive toward the upward call of God in Christ Jesus may enter.

> Not that I have already obtained, or am already perfected; but I press on, that I may lay hold of that for which Christ Jesus has also laid hold of me. Brethren, I do not count myself to have apprehended; but one thing I do, forgetting those things which are behind and reaching forward to those things which are ahead, I press toward the goal for the prize of the upward call of God in Christ Jesus (Phil. 3:12–14).

CHAPTER 2

Dreams

A dream consists of images passing through the mind during sleep. Joseph, one of Jacob's sons, dreamed prophetic dreams and was able to interpret the dreams of others.

> Now Joseph had a dream and he told it to his brothers … "There we were, binding sheaves in the field. Then behold, my sheaf arose and also stood upright; and indeed your sheaves stood all around and bowed down to my sheaf" (Gen. 37:5–7).

His brothers interpreted the dream as follows:

> And his brothers said to him, "Shall you indeed reign over us? Or shall you indeed have dominion over us?" (Gen. 37:8).

Then Joseph told them another dream.

> Then he dreamed still another dream and told it to his brothers, and said, "Look, I have dreamed another dream. And this time, the sun, the moon, and the eleven stars bowed down to me" (Gen. 37:9).

This dream upset his family and caused his father to rebuke him.

> So he told it to his father and his brothers; and his father rebuked him and said to him, "What is this dream that you have dreamed? Shall your mother and I and your brothers indeed come to bow down to the earth before you?" (Gen. 37:10).

Both of these dreams were prophetic in nature, as they pointed to the time when Joseph was appointed second in command to the pharaoh of Egypt. While in prison, Joseph interpreted a couple of dreams that gained him audience with the pharaoh. He interpreted the pharaoh's dreams and predicted seven years of plenty and seven years of drought, which won him favor with the pharaoh. Joseph's earlier dreams came true when he invited his family to come to Egypt because of the drought, and his position of authority demonstrated his rule over his family.

In the story of Gideon, one of his men had a dream, and another interpreted the dream. When he overheard the two men discussing the dream, Gideon used the interpretation in his decision to attack the camp of Midian.

> And when Gideon had come, there was a man telling a dream to his companion. He said, "I have had a dream: To my surprise, a loaf of barley bread

tumbled into the camp of Midian; it came to a tent and struck it so that it fell and overturned, and the tent collapsed." Then his companion answered and said, "This is nothing else but the sword of Gideon the son of Joash, a man of Israel! Into his hand God has delivered Midian and the whole camp." And so it was, when Gideon heard the telling of the dream and its interpretation, that he worshiped. He returned to the camp of Israel, and said, "Arise, for the Lord has delivered the camp of Midian into your hand" (Judg. 7:13–14).

In the case of Daniel, King Nebuchadnezzar wanted the interpreter to not only interpret his dream but tell him the dream as well.

> Then the king gave the command to call the magicians, the astrologers, the sorcerers, and the Chaldeans to tell the king his dreams. So they came and stood before the king and the king said to them, "I have had a dream, and my spirit is anxious to know the dream." Then the Chaldeans spoke to the king in Aramaic, "O king, live forever! Tell your servants the dream, and we will give the interpretation." The king answered and said to the Chaldeans, "My decision is firm: if you do not make known the dream to me, and its interpretation, you shall be cut in pieces, and your houses shall be made an ash heap. However, if you tell the dream and its interpretation, you shall receive from me gifts, rewards, and great honor.

Therefore tell me the dream and its interpretation" (Dan. 2:3–6).

Daniel told the king his dream and its interpretation.

You, O king, were watching; and behold, a great image! This great image, whose splendor was excellent, stood before you; and its form was awesome. This image's head was of fine gold, its chest and arms of silver, its belly and thighs of bronze, its legs of iron, its feet partly of iron and partly of clay. You watched while a stone was cut out without hands, which struck the image on its feet of iron and clay, and broke them in pieces. Then the iron, the clay, the bronze, the silver, and the gold were crushed together, and became like chaff from the summer threshing floors; the wind carried them away so that no trace of them was found. And the stone that struck the image became a great mountain and filled the whole earth (Dan. 2:31–35).

Following this, Daniel interpreted the dream. (See Daniel 2:36–45.)

Interpreting dreams is similar to interpreting visions. For example, I dreamed of a tsunami striking the west coast. I saw this as a disaster of some sort hitting our nation. A day or so after the dream, the stock market experienced a major downward correction. To my surprise, a TV commentator used the words "economic tsunami" to describe the situation.

A couple of other dreams told of future events in detail. While on a research ship, I dreamed that I was involved in the mobilization of another research ship. I was extremely upset that I was doing this because I didn't want to get involved in any more sea trips. I immediately woke up and was very agitated. I remembered the dream in detail. Upon returning home, my supervisor called me into his office and begged me to assist in the mobilization of a research ship. I reluctantly accepted the task. My friend who photographed many such events wanted to take pictures of the operation. I took him to an area located on the second story of an abandoned building. As I looked at the activity going on around the ship, to my surprise, the images (in particular the colors) were the same as what I had dreamed while aboard the other ship. The interesting thing is that while aboard this second ship, I had another dream that foretold an event that was going to take place on the trip. Lo and behold, this event took place in such detail that I came to the conclusion that the Lord wanted me on that trip.

Many dreams appear to be warnings. They point to disasters, such as economic crises, family issues, or major issues within the body of Christ. The warnings usually mean for me to brace myself or prepare for what is to come. They are warnings to others as well.

CHAPTER 3

THE PURPOSE OF A PROPHET

Prophets serve several purposes. In the Old Testament, their main purposes were to serve as watchmen and warn the people when they are straying from the ways of God and to tell the people the consequences of not heeding warnings and turning from their wicked ways.

> Son of man, I have made you a watchman for the house of Israel; therefore hear a word from My mouth, and give them warning from Me (Ezek. 3:17).

In the case of Moses, prophetic words gave direction to the people in the areas of building a tabernacle, the order of priesthood, what foods to eat and not eat, how to deal with diseases, etc. The Lord also used prophets to give direction to Israel when they were confronted with the enemy.

> Now Deborah, a prophetess, the wife of Lapidoth, was judging Israel at that time ... Then she sent

> and called for Barak the son of Abinoam from Kedesh in Naphtali, and said to him, "Has not the Lord God of Israel commanded, 'Go and deploy troops at Mount Tabor; take with you ten thousand men of the sons of Naphtali and of the sons of Zebulun'" (Judg. 4:4, 6).

Then there were prophets like Daniel and Joseph who could interpret dreams and foretell future events.

In the New Testament, we have one main Prophet, Jesus. In the book of Revelation, John appears as a major prophet of future events. Aside from what is written, God provides truth concerning His ways by the Holy Spirit. Since the Lord wants us to develop within ourselves the mind of Christ, listening to what the Spirit is saying is very important.

> But the Helper, the Holy Spirit, whom the Father will send in My name, He will teach you all things, and bring to your remembrance all things that I said to you (John 14:26).

This is where those who are filled with the Holy Spirit come into play. The Lord will speak to those with the appropriate gifts to teach truth. Today's prophets are not just limited to teaching. They exhort people to persevere in the faith, warn them about straying from the Lord, and tell them the consequences of not listening to the Lord. The ultimate goal of visions and dreams is to add to the glory of God. Remember, any true word from a prophet does not contradict Scripture.

A good guideline to follow is to identify the characteristics of Jesus and contrast them with the character of the devil. The characteristics of Jesus are peace, gentleness, love, compassion, mercy, truth, order, and knowledge and understanding of the

Father. The devil's character is one of chaos, destruction, hate, error, torture, tormenting, ignorance of the Father, being a liar, harshness, and being a promoter of terror and anguish.

Basically, people become like the god they worship. Those who worship Jesus become like Him. Those who worship Satan become like him. Those who have the mindset of murdering or causing terror and chaos have the mindset of Satan. The followers of Satan are liars and deceivers. They will torment and torture people. Any religion that has this mindset follows Satan. Jesus is the way, the truth, and the life. No one comes to the Father except through Him. Jesus is the Savior. Satan is the destroyer.

A prophet has a great deal of responsibility. He or she must take time to listen to the Lord, interpret what is being said, and then inform fellow Christians what the Lord is saying. If the prophet hears and does not speak to the people, the Lord will not be pleased.

> But if the watchman sees the sword coming and does not blow the trumpet, and the people are not warned, and the sword comes and takes any person from among them, he is taken away in his iniquity; but his blood I will require at the watchman's hand. So you, son of man: I have made you a watchman for the house of Israel; therefore you shall hear a word from My mouth and warn them for Me. When I say to the wicked, "O wicked man, you shall surely die!" and you do not speak to warn the wicked from his way, that wicked man shall die in his iniquity; but his blood I will require at your hand. Nevertheless if you warn the wicked to turn from his way, and he does not turn from his way, he shall die in his

iniquity; but you have delivered your soul (Ezek. 33:6–9).

This places a huge burden on the prophet, not only to speak to the people but also to speak the truth.

It's important for a prophet to be under a covering. The church pastor/leader is the prophet's covering. The church leader should be wise enough to discern the validity of a prophetic saying and take responsibility to pass on what appears to be a valid word for the people. When a prophet receives a word that is meant for an individual, it's usually best to get permission from the church leader before doing so. There were times when I pulled people aside and told them what I felt the Lord was saying about their situation, but a decision to do this should be made on a case-by-case basis. The main thing is to not embarrass anyone in front of other people.

Christian friends who know my gifting will ask me if the Lord has said anything concerning a prayer request. If the Lord has spoken, I will generally relay what I felt the Lord said. If I have a question about interpretation or the message in general, I usually will not share it at that time and sometimes I will never share it.

CHAPTER 4

CULTS

The gift of visions and dreams must be handled very carefully. Misusing the gift can lead to a number of issues. It can open the mind to demonic influences, inflate one's ego, and even lead to a cult. In these cases, the gift is at great risk of being taken away.

Prophetic visions and dreams are generally accepted in the charismatic circle. Outside of this circle, these gifts are met with skepticism and are often labeled as satanic. The organization that sponsors the gift will be labeled as a cult.

From a Christian standpoint, a cult is any religious group that deviates from the fundamental teachings of the historic, Bible-based Christian faith. A new religious movement on its way to becoming a denomination headed by a charismatic leader and viewed as a spiritually innovative group will often be labeled as a cult. When the Anabaptists broke away from the Lutherans and introduced "baptism by full immersion," the Lutherans labeled them as a cult. When the Pentecostal Church introduced speaking in tongues and experiencing charismatic gifts, they were labeled as a cult.

Worldly as well as radical Christian cults tend to prey on people's insecurities and emotional and sometimes physical needs. These weaknesses make people vulnerable to spiritual movements. Everyone wants to feel loved and cared for.

Worldly cults often use religious terms and will use the guise of religion to seduce people into the organization. Once in, they weave a web that prevents members from accessing any independence, free thought, or ability to analyze. They will use brainwashing, which is a very powerful and seductive tool, to control their members.

A visionary within the church will attract elements from all walks of life. What may start out as an innocent bonding to a spiritual movement can soon turn into an unpleasant experience. Those who possess the gift of visions and dreams need to be on guard for this. An inflated ego combined with a following can eventually lead to manipulating people, both from an individualistic and a congregational point of view.

The People's Temple led by Jim Jones is an excellent example of this. The lack of awareness and education led 912 followers to their death in Jonestown, Guyana. Cult leaders use deception and thought control to influence their followers. Most cults are led by charismatic leaders who are authoritarian in nature. Cult leaders put pressure on followers to lose touch with their old personality and lifestyle and force them to cut off ties to relatives and friends. With a little treachery, leaders pull religious elements out of context, twist them a bit, and then use them as powerful tools for convincing followers that their doctrinal beliefs are in tune with God's overall scheme of things. They convince their followers that everyone else is wrong.

Cults tend to focus on young, immature, and uninformed people and draw from portions of other religions or philosophies or even fabricate a connection to aliens from outer space.

Heaven's Gate was a UFO cult in which two people portrayed themselves as the two witnesses spoken of in the Bible (Rev. 11:3). They went around the country giving talks about their beliefs. They combined Christian doctrine with elements of science fiction, particularly travel to other worlds and dimensions. They convinced their followers that the planet earth was about to be destroyed and that the only way of escape was to leave. When the comet Hale-Bopp appeared, they convinced their followers that the comet was followed by a spaceship that would take them to a higher dimension, and that by committing suicide when the comet Hale-Bopp was at its brightest, they could reach the spaceship. Thirty-nine of their followers committed suicide.

The gift of visions and dreams can draw a following. It is important to stay close to the holy Scriptures and let the message of the cross dominate one's doctrine. God must be the one to receive the glory of visions and dreams. The goal of a Christian is to develop within him or herself the mind of Christ. Visions and dreams will support this concept and exhort followers to persevere in the faith. Some prophetic visions may warn Christians of events that are going to take place. This allows them to prepare for the future. However, a prophet's actions should not contradict the Scriptures.

CHAPTER 5

Knowledge, Understanding, and Wisdom

Interpreting and applying prophetic visions involves three key words found throughout Scripture: knowledge, understanding and wisdom.

> For the Lord gives *wisdom*; from His mouth come *knowledge* and *understanding* (Prov. 2:6).

Knowledge is awareness of facts.
Understanding is the interpretation of facts in order to comprehend, perceive, discern, recognize or find the meaning behind something that was said or something that has happened.
Wisdom is the ability to take knowledge and apply it to life's opportunities, challenges, and circumstances.
The relationship between knowledge, understanding, and wisdom is shown in the following table:

	Definition
Knowledge	Possession of facts
Understanding	Interpretation of facts
Wisdom	Application of facts

These words are used extensively in the book of Proverbs. Reading Proverbs and replacing these words with their definitions will bring increased enlightenment.

Examples that demonstrate the relationship between knowledge and understanding can be found in the parables of the sower and the wheat and tares recounted in Matthew 13. Jesus interpreted both of these parables for his disciples so they could understand what He was saying.

The parable of the sower is as follows:

> Then He spoke many things to them in parables, saying: "Behold, a sower went out to sow. And as he sowed, some seed fell by the wayside; and the birds came and devoured them. Some fell on stony places, where they did not have much earth; and they immediately sprang up because they had no depth of earth. But when the sun was up they were scorched, and because they had no root they withered away. And some fell among thorns, and the thorns sprang up and choked them. But others fell on good ground and yielded a crop: some a hundredfold, some sixty, some thirty" (Matt. 13:3–8).

Having read the above passage, the reader now has knowledge (or facts) concerning the parable of the sower. The disciples heard the parable but did not understand it. Jesus gave them the understanding (interpretation) in the following verses:

> Therefore hear the parable of the sower: "When anyone hears the word of the kingdom, and does not understand it, then the wicked one comes and snatches away what was sown in his heart. This is he who received seed by the wayside. But he who received the seed on stony places, this is he who hears the word and immediately receives it with joy; yet he has no root in himself, but endures only for a while. For when tribulation or persecution arises because of the word, immediately he stumbles. Now he who received seed among the thorns is he who hears the word, and the cares of this world and the deceitfulness of riches choke the word, and he becomes unfruitful. But he who received seed on the good ground is he who hears the word and understands it, whom indeed bears fruit and produces: some a hundredfold, some sixty, some thirty" (Matt. 13:18–23).

The interpretation of the symbols/types is as follows:

Seed	word of the kingdom
Wayside	lack of understanding
Birds	wicked one
Stony places	lack of endurance
Sun scorched	tribulation
Withered away	stumbles

Thorns	cares of the world, deceitfulness of riches
Choked them	unfruitful
Good ground	understands it
Yielded a crop	bears fruit and produces

From the above parable, knowing that understanding the word of the kingdom and bearing fruit is of importance, a wise person will apply that to his or her Christian walk.

The parable of the wheat and tares is as follows:

> Another parable He put forth to them, saying: "The kingdom of heaven is like a man who sowed good seed in his field; but while men slept, his enemy came and sowed tares among the wheat and went his way. But when the grain had sprouted and produced a crop, then the tares also appeared. So the servants of the owner came and said to him, 'Sir, did you not sow good seed in your field? How then does it have tares?' He said to them, 'An enemy has done this.' The servants said to him, 'Do you want us then to go and gather them up?' But he said, 'No, lest while you gather up the tares you also uproot the wheat with them. Let both grow together until the harvest, and at the time of harvest I will say to the reapers, "First gather together the tares and bind them in bundles to burn them, but gather the wheat into my barn""" (Matt. 13:24-30).

Here again, having read the above passage, the reader has knowledge (or facts) concerning the parable of the wheat and tares. Jesus gave them the understanding (interpretation) in the following verses:

> Then Jesus sent the multitude away and went into the house. And His disciples came to Him, saying, "Explain to us the parable of the tares of the field." He answered and said to them: "He who sows the good seed is the Son of Man. The field is the world, the good seeds are the sons of the kingdom, but the tares are the sons of the wicked one. The enemy who sowed them is the devil, the harvest is the end of the age, and the reapers are the angels. Therefore as the tares are gathered and burned in the fire, so it will be at the end of this age. The Son of Man will send out His angels, and they will gather out of His kingdom all things that offend, and those who practice lawlessness, and will cast them into the furnace of fire. There will be wailing and gnashing of teeth. Then the righteous will shine forth as the sun in the kingdom of their Father ..." (Matt. 13:36–43).

The interpretation of the symbols/types is as follows:

Sower of good seed	Son of Man
Field	world
Good seeds	sons of the kingdom
Tares	sons of the wicked one
Enemy	the devil
Harvest	at the end of this age

Reapers	angels
Bind tares/burn	offenders/lawless are cast into a furnace of fire.
Wheat in barn	righteous enter Father's kingdom.

Jesus explained parables to His disciples so they would know the mysteries concerning the kingdom of heaven.

> And the disciples came and said to Him, "Why do You speak to them in parables?" He answered and said to them, "Because it has been given to you to know the mysteries of the kingdom of heaven, but to them it has not been given" (Matt. 13:10–11).

The source of understanding is the Holy Spirit.

> How that by revelation knowledge He made known to me the mystery ... by which when you read, you may understand my knowledge in the mystery of Christ, which in other ages was not made known to the sons of men, as it has now been revealed by the Spirit to His holy apostles and prophets. (Eph. 3:3–5).

An example of the Holy Spirit providing understanding was when the apostle John introduced John the Baptist. John 1:5 states:

> And the light shines in the darkness, and the darkness did not comprehend it.

In verses 6 and 7, John the Baptist comes along bearing witness of the light. He understood the light. What was different about John the Baptist that he was able to comprehend the light and others couldn't?

> He [John the Baptist] will also be filled with the Holy Spirit, even from his mother's womb (Luke 1:15).

John the Baptist was filled with the Holy Spirit, and as such, he was able to comprehend the light. Understanding is recognizing truth in the midst of darkness.

God gives wisdom in the form of knowledge and understanding.

> For the Lord gives wisdom; from His mouth come knowledge and understanding (Prov. 2:6).

The prophet will receive a dark saying from the Lord as knowledge. He or she will understand (interpret) the dark saying with the help of the Lord. As Proverbs 1:5–6 says:

> A man of understanding will attain wise counsel,
> to understand a proverb and an enigma, the words
> of the wise and their riddles.

In a vision or a dream, the symbols are facts. Interpreting these symbols clarifies what is being said. This clarification becomes a higher level of knowledge. Acting on this knowledge (applying it to your lifestyle) is wisdom. Knowledge and understanding of the ways of God infuse life into those who have died to the world and have made a decision to follow Christ.

A visionary will receive knowledge, interpret it (apply understanding), and wisely apply it for the benefit of mankind and to add to the glory of God.

CHAPTER 6

TRAINING

There don't appear to be any schools available to train prophets. I rely on the Holy Spirit to help me understand prophetic dreams and visions. I asked for help from church leadership, but it was futile. My leaders didn't know how to handle the visions because they hadn't experienced them themselves or weren't trained in their seminaries on how to deal with prophetic communications of these types. Church leaders tend to avoid this realm with the same fear of not wanting to deal with the book of Revelation. However, a church small group leader and one of my Sunday school teachers did take an interest in the gift of prophetic dreams and visions.

My first vision consisted of a brown and white side view of someone's head. I was more excited about seeing a vision than trying to interpret what it meant. At first, I didn't write down the visions. It wasn't until I started to receive them on a regular basis that I decided to write them down.

My first visions were in black and white, and the objects were fixed in position. Eventually, they began to appear in vivid color. I remember receiving a vision of a red rose. The details of the rose were perfect. The first visions I had that demonstrated motion were in black and white and shades of gray. My first vision of this type was of a white horse and a rider galloping at a fairly high speed. Eventually, I saw motion in color.

The most interesting vision I've had showing motion occurred when I sat down at the dinner table just after returning from a morning church service. I closed my eyes, and immediately I saw what appeared to be a column of legionnaires riding horses at a distance. The background was brown and white color, with hills behind the riders. It was a desert/wilderness scene. The lead rider was carrying a triangular flag. The riders were moving from left to right, and eventually, they came around and passed in front of me. As the lead rider, who appeared to be the captain of the group, passed in front of me, he stopped, turned his head toward me, and stared right at me, as if to say, "Are you going to join me?" I interpreted the flag as identifying the group as the Lord's army, with the triangular shape standing for the trinity (the Father, Son, and Holy Spirit). I interpreted the leader as the Captain of Hosts.

At times the Spirit gives me the interpretation of a figure or scene during the vision. Other times if I ask the Lord for an interpretation during the vision, He will provide it. Many times I get hung up on an interpretation and put it on the back burner. One time the Lord gave me some instruction on interpretation through the following dream.

Dream Involving Training
When: March 7, 1990
Description: I was looking at a black-and-white picture that was dark, with a few items barely discernable. The scene was that of a neighborhood with a street lamp, a car, residences etc. I attempted

to make out the background by first concentrating on the signal light. I could see the top two lights but not the bottom light. As I tilted the picture, the scene became clearer. I got the impression that I was in a school and Pastor Pamela Truscott was my teacher. She gave me a test to determine certain things from the picture. It seems that I was under pressure to finish the test within a certain time limit. I had a difficult time under these restrictions. It seems someone hinted to me one of the answers. I got that answer wrong, and a point was taken off before I continued to take the test.

Interpretation: The black-and-white picture was a word spoken in a dark language. In real life, Pastor Pamela was teaching me hermeneutics, the art and science of interpreting the communication of God to man. Tilting the picture and seeing more objects meant that to get a better understanding of the picture, one must view it from another perspective. I should not let the pressure of time force an interpretation. I should let the Holy Spirit reveal the interpretation and not let others influence the interpretation or errors would be introduced.

It's important to write down every detail of a vision. The background of the vision is equally important. For example, if a church leader is preaching on the Lord's army during a Sunday morning service and you receive a vision involving an army, the two may be related. However, not all visions or dreams will reflect the topic of discussion in the background. To force a vision to fit a particular discussion topic puts the Lord in a box. The door must be open to allow the Lord to speak freely on any subject He chooses.

Another form of communication that can be buried in a vision is the use of a pantomime. My pastor mentioned that some prophets spoke in this fashion. One early morning before heading to work, I stopped by the church to join a prayer group. This prayer group arose early in the morning to pray before going to work. During the group prayer, the Lord showed me hand and arm movements to demonstrate to the group. It was one of my earlier visions. The Spirit also interpreted the movements for me so I could show the group what each movement meant. The following vision summarizes what took place:

> **Vision with a Pantomime**
> **When**: May 16, 1988
> **Where**: MBCF
> **Description:** I saw the arm of a warrior. The fist was clenched, and the fingers and hand were angular, denoting a fist of steel. There was a long wristband on the arm, like that of a warrior. As I watched, the left hand came over and felt the right bicep. Next, the arms crossed at the chest. The thought of protection came to mind, that the Lord will protect us. Then the arms raised, a large loaf of bread appeared in the hands, and the bread was drawn to the mouth. My thought was that the Lord was going to feed us an abundance of bread. The word "abundance" was emphasized. (Interestingly, a second later, the prayer leader mentioned the word "bread," as if it was meant

for confirmation.) I felt the Lord wanted me to act this out. I did so as I explained the vision.

Interpretation: I will give you strength and protection and provide for you.

Since that time, I have never used this form of presenting a vision. I got the impression that the Lord was demonstrating that the use of pantomime was a valid method of presenting prophecies, as stated by the pastor in his sermon.

One of the problems with recording visions is that time tends to cause one to forget the details of what the object looked like. Using color pencils, I sketched out a couple of visions. A few years later, as I perused my book of visions, I marveled at how important the sketches were. It was like night and day when reading the visions. Although I'm not an artist, the sketches really made a difference in reminding me what the objects looked like at the time of the vision.

Some visions are so vivid that I can recall them twenty or so years later. A recent vision really stood out. I can still see it today. I asked the Lord what His thoughts were on my recently published book, *Genesis 1*. The following vision is what I received.

Vision of the Ancient Lamp

When: September 8, 2010

Where: Home, Tucson

Background: Before taking a nap, I had asked the Lord what He thought of my recently published book and received a vision upon waking from the nap.

Description: I saw what appeared to be an ancient relic. It is a bit difficult to describe. It had a spherical center with a narrow neck on the top and bottom. The very top and bottom were square. It appeared brown in color. The front of the spherical section broke into several large chards (pieces). It appeared to be made of fired clay. As the pieces fell away, the lens of a light appeared, like that of a car headlight. The thought came to mind that it was a lamp/light of some sort encapsulated in a clay relic. Then I saw what appeared to be statues (I believe there were three of them) of ancient warriors/kings something like those in ancient Babylon. They were tall and appeared brownish in color.

Interpretation: The revealing of something that has been hidden for thousands of years in the area or time of ancient Babylon or the Middle East.

Comment: I wouldn't have thought that the concept introduced in my book (*Genesis 1*) was that old. Perhaps the content is lost or hidden knowledge.

Symbols

There are numerous symbols used in visions. Symbolism is a language within itself. Compiling a symbol-to-English language list would be like generating a dictionary. The following list contains some common symbols encountered in my visions. The meaning of some symbols may vary according to the context of the vision. Remember, the interpretation of a vision depends on the prophet. The interpretation of a symbol by one person may be totally different from that of another person.

Basket—gatherings
Bottle—the body

Butterfly—renewal
Caldron—turmoil
Candle—preacher, church leader
Chains—bondage
Dark clouds—turmoil on its way
Ear of a cup—hear what the Lord has to say
Earthquake—shaking, warning
Elephant—beast
Flame—Word of God, judgment
Ghostly hand—hand of the Spirit
Handicap logo—handicapped
Hat—covering
Light—Word of God
Lion—courage, boldness
Locust—devouring
Microphone—speak to the congregation
Microscope—examine closely
Mixer—stir up
Pen—write
River—flow of the Holy Spirit
Ring—marriage
Satellite antenna—communication; receive, transmit, or two-way
Scissors—cut, cut out
Sea—world
Snow—hard times
Telephone—calling
Tidal wave—disaster or crisis from the world
Triangle—Trinity; Father, Son, and Holy Spirit
Umbrella—covering, protection
Water—Holy Spirit
White hand—hand of the Lord

Wine glass—Christian, body
Wine—Word of God, blood
Wolves—devourers
Wood—humanity

Numbers

There are many principles used in interpreting Scripture. The one that stands out the most when interpreting dreams and visions is the numerical principle. This principle recognizes the symbolic significances of numbers involved in interpretation of Scripture. The following list is what I use for interpreting visions and dreams. It is slightly different than what other theologians may use. An explanation of any differences will be shown.

One—there is only one God.

> Hear, O Israel: The Lord our God, the Lord is one! (Deut. 6:4).

> There is one body and one Spirit, just as you were called in one hope of your calling; one Lord, one faith, one baptism; one God and Father of all, who is above all, and through all, and in you all (Eph. 4:4–6).

Two—number of witness or testimony; knowledge and understanding

> It is also written in your law that the testimony of two men is true.
> I am One who bears witness of Myself, and the Father who sent Me bears witness of Me (John 8:17–18).

> For the Lord gives wisdom; From His mouth come knowledge and understanding (Prov. 2:6).

Three—number of the Godhead; the trinity

> Go therefore and make disciples of all the nations, baptizing them in the name of the Father and of the Son and of the Holy Spirit (Matt. 28:19).

Four—number of the earth, world

> After these things I saw four angels standing at the four corners of the earth, holding the four winds of the earth, that the wind should not blow on the earth, on the sea, or on any tree (Rev. 7:1).

Five—five-fold ministry, kingdom of heaven

> And He Himself gave some to be apostles, some prophets, some evangelists, and some pastors and teachers (Eph. 4:11).

In my book *Genesis 1—The Design and Plan for the Kingdom of Heaven*, I point out that the first five days of creation, in an allegorical sense, are the design and plan of a school where students have the opportunity to develop within themselves the mind of Christ.

Six—number of man

> Then God said, "Let Us make man in Our image, according to Our likeness; let them have dominion over the fish of the sea, over the birds of the air, and over the cattle, over all the earth and over every creeping thing that creeps on the earth ... So the evening and the morning were the sixth day (Gen. 1:26, 31).

Seven—divine completeness, seven days of creation, Sabbath

> And on the seventh day God ended His work which He had done, and He rested on the seventh day from all His work which He had done(Genesis 2:2).

Eight—salvation with respect to Jesus, destruction with respect to the anti-Christ

Jesus in Greek means "Savior." This is a fitting name, as it is through Him we receive salvation.

> And she will bring forth a Son, and you shall call His name Jesus, for He will save His people from their sins (Matt. 1:21).

Using the Greek ciphered number system, the number that represents the name "Jesus" is 888.

	1	2	3	4	5	6	7	8	9
1	A	B	Γ	Δ	E	F	Z	H	Θ
10	I	K	Λ	M	N	Ξ	O	Π	Q
100	P	Σ	T	Y	Φ	X	Ψ	Ω	S

I	=	10
H	=	8
Σ	=	200
O	=	70
Y	=	400
Σ	=	<u>200</u>
	Total	888

It is interesting to note that Jesus was the Son of David, who was the eighth son of Jesse. The number eight is associated with salvation. This reasoning is supported in part by the salvation of Noah and his family during the great flood; eight people (Noah, his wife, his three sons, and his sons' wives) were saved aboard the ark.

> Who formerly were disobedient, when once the Divine longsuffering waited in the days of Noah, while the ark was being prepared, in which a few, that is, *eight souls, were saved* through water (1 Peter 3:20).

As mentioned, the beast is associated with destruction.

> And the beast that was, and is not, is himself also the *eighth*, and is of the seven, and is going to

perdition [eternal damnation, destruction, hell] (Rev. 17:11).

Nine—Holy Spirit; nine gifts and nine fruits of the Holy Spirit are mentioned.

> But the manifestation of the Spirit is given to each one for the profit of all: for to one is given the *word of wisdom* through the Spirit, to another the *word of knowledge* through the same Spirit, to another *faith* by the same Spirit, to another gifts of *healings* by the same Spirit, to another the *working of miracles*, to another *prophecy*, to another *discerning of spirits*, to another *different kinds of tongues*, to another the *interpretation of tongues* (1 Cor. 12:7–10).

> But the fruit of the Spirit is *love, joy, peace, longsuffering, kindness, goodness, faithfulness, gentleness, self-control.* Against such there is no law (Gal. 5:22–23).

Ten—law (Ten Commandments)

Eleven—incompleteness

There were twelve apostles. When Judas betrayed the Lord and departed from the group of twelve, the remaining apostles cast lots to bring the number back to twelve.

> And they cast their lots, and the lot fell on Matthias. And he was numbered with the eleven apostles (Acts 1:26).

Twelve—twelve tribes of Israel, twelve apostles, true doctrine

The number twelve has its real importance in the area of preserving the true Christian doctrine. When the apostles cast lots to choose a replacement for Judas Iscariot, their criteria were having been with the Lord from the beginning and witnessing the resurrection.

> Therefore, of these men who have accompanied us all the time that the Lord Jesus went in and out among us, beginning from the baptism of John to that day when He was taken up from us, one of these must become a witness with us of His resurrection (Acts 1:21–22).

The apostles were empowered to preserve the doctrine. If someone claimed to be an apostle, he was to be tested.

> I know your works, your labor, your patience, and that you cannot bear those who are evil. And you have tested those who say they are apostles and are not, and have found them liars (Rev. 2:2).

Thirteen—rebellion

Nimrod was in the thirteenth generation from Adam. He founded Babel in which the famous Tower of Babel was built. This tower was considered to be a rebellious act against God. The number thirteen is considered by the superstitious to be unlucky. There's little biblical support for this number. When I see the number in dreams, it appears to represent rebellion or darkness.

Twenty-four—number of priestly courses, number of elders

First Chronicles 24:1–19 lists the names of twenty-four priests who were the sons of Eleazar and Ithamar and who were to minister in the house of the Lord. The following lists the priests in the order given in the Bible and the interpretations of the names are taken from various study guides[1,2]. Not all study guides agree with some of the interpretations.

    Jehoiarib—Jehovah will contend
    Jedaiah—Jehovah has known
    Harim—dedicated to God
    Seorim—barley grains
    Malchijah—king of God
    Mijamin—from the right hand (fortunate)
    Hakkoz—thorn, pricking
    Abijah—worshiper of Jah or God
    Jeshuah—he will save
    Shecaniah—dweller with God
    Eliahshib—God will restore
    Jakim—he will raise
    Huppah—canopy, defense, covered, protection
    Jeshebeab—people will return (father's place)
    Bilgah—bursting forth, first born, cheerfulness
    Immer—talkative, prominent, lamb
    Hezir—returning home
    Happizzez—hasty
    Pethahiah—God has opened, freed by God
    Jehezekel—God will strengthen
    Jachin—he will establish
    Gamul—rewarded
    Delaiah—God has delivered
    Maaziah—protection, God is a refuge

From these meanings, in the order given above and with my fill-ins, the following is written:

> *God will contend* with a company of people *He has known* who are *dedicated to Him*. He will send the *bread of life from His right hand* who will become their *King*. The King will *prod* the people to *worship the Lord their God*. He will bring salvation to the people who *dwell with God*. *God will restore* the lost sheep, *raise* them up, and be their *canopy of protection*. Those who *return to the Father* will become the *firstfruits* who will *figure prominently* with the Lamb. Therefore, encourage the people to hastily return home, for *God will free them* from bondage, *strengthen* them, and *establish* them. God will *reward* those He has *delivered* with a place of *refuge in Him*.

Note: The above interpretation was something I discovered while writing my thesis. I haven't seen this written any place else.

The high points here are that God intends to bring the lost sheep home and that those who return home will figure prominently with the Lamb. When seen in a vision or dream, the number twenty-four can be translated to mean the lost sheep. This may explain the twenty-four elders mentioned in Revelation 4.

> Around the throne were twenty-four thrones, and on the thrones I saw twenty-four elders sitting, clothed in white robes; and they had crowns of gold on their heads (Rev. 4:4).

John referred to Christians as kings and priests.

> And has made us kings and priests to His God and Father, to Him be glory and dominion forever and ever. Amen (Rev. 1:6).

The twenty-four elders represent those who are the firstfruits and who figure prominently with the Lord.

The following example is a vision in which three different numbers were used.

> **Vision of the Drinking Glasses**
> **When**: May 26, 1994
> **Where**: Leadership meeting at MBCF
> **Description**: I saw two crystal-clear drinking glasses. There was a lit candle in each of them. Immediately to the left of them, I saw three more crystal-clear drinking glasses. Each of them contained a lit candle. The three drinking glasses disappeared, and immediately, six empty clear-crystal drinking glasses appeared and passed between the two glasses with the lit candles.
> **Interpretation**:

Two glasses with lit candles—two witnesses
Three glasses with lit candles—Father, Son, and Holy Spirit
Six glasses without lit candles—unsaved people

> **Summary**: Leadership must focus on bearing witness of the Word to the unsaved in the name of the Father, Son, and Holy Spirit.

> Go therefore and make disciples of all the nations, baptizing them in the name of the Father and of the Son and of the Holy Spirit, teaching them to observe all things that I have commanded you; and lo, I am with you always, even to the end of the age. Amen (Matt. 28:19–20).

> **Comment**: I suspect that the vision was designed to bring the leadership meeting into focus.

I hope the reader will seek the gift of visions and be able to understand them from the examples shown in this book. Keep in mind that the Holy Spirit will serve as your tutor.

> But the Helper, the Holy Spirit, whom the Father will send in My name, He will teach you all things, and bring to your remembrance all things that I said to you (John 14:26).

The Lord spoke to His disciples in a figurative language called parables. It is not unusual for the Lord to speak to us today in a figurative language. The Holy Spirit will serve as your Helper to aid you in understanding visions.

(1) Joan Comay and Ronald Brownrigg, *Who's Who in the Bible*, Bonanza Books, New York, NY, 1980
(2) J. Packer, Merrill Tenney, and William White, *The Bible Almanac*, Guideposts, Carmel, NY, 1980

CHAPTER 7

Prayer

Most of my visions were received during group prayer time. This emphasizes the importance of prayer in our life. Prayer is of vital importance and quite beneficial in many aspects. It will lower work stress levels, heal the sick, solve problems, rescue people from danger, help spread the Word, and promote church growth.

> For where two or three are gathered together in My name, I am there in the midst of them (Matt. 18:20).

My favorite gathering is with a group of men on Saturday mornings at Faith Chapel in Spring Valley, California. It is a time of praising God, praying for others, and laying on of hands for such things as healings, jobs, finances, and countless other issues. Many of my prayers, as well as the prayers of others, were answered following these prayer meetings. I also received a significant number of visions during these meetings.

Now that I'm living in Tucson, Arizona, I only get to join the group when I'm visiting the area on a Saturday.

I received the following vision at one of the Saturday-morning prayer meetings, and it demonstrates the necessity of gathering together and praying:

> **Vision of the Quad Cane**
> **When**: March 3, 2001
> **Where**: Faith Chapel
> **Background**: I was seeking the Lord for a word while the brethren were laying on hands and praying for individuals.
> **Description**: I saw a cane with a footed bottom (quad cane) similar to those used by handicapped people. It immediately reminded me of a lady I met the night before who had arthritis and was scheduled for hip surgery. She was using a similar cane for getting around. I told my wife that I would pray for her during the men's prayer meeting. The vision reminded me to pray for her. I brought it to the attention of the group, and we prayed for her. I felt the presence of the Lord in a strong way. I felt His presence even stronger when we prayed for a lady who had cancer.

I've had hands laid on me for healing with positive results. One healing was instantaneous. Although I make no claim to having the gift of healing, I've laid hands on some folks with positive results. People tell me that my hand(s) feel extremely hot when I pray and lay hands on them for healing or when I place my hands on people's shoulders during prayer sessions and ask the Lord to simply bless them.

One evening while I was attending Mission Bay Christian Fellowship (it may have been Restoration Temple at that time), Pastor Pamela was preaching and gave a testimony of how she prayed over a growth of some sort on her hand or arm (I can't recall which). Shortly thereafter, the growth disappeared. I was working in the sound booth that evening and said to myself, *If the Lord can do that simple thing for her, why can't He do it for me?* I looked at a cauliflower wart on my left forearm, laid my right hand on it, and demanded that it go away in the name of Jesus. The wart had been around for a long time. The next day, the wart was gone. Only a little white spot remained. Eventually the white spot disappeared as well.

I have had countless work issues resolved by simply praying on the way to work or while at work. One method to my prayers is to include the Lord in my requests. It was how can *we* solve this problem, not how can *I* solve the problem. If I had an unresolved issue at work, I would pray about it before going to bed at night. Many times the issue would be resolved before getting to work. This made for a low stress level.

There are times when the Lord will place a thought on my mind or perhaps speak to me in a dream that is associated with rescuing someone from danger. For example, I once had a dream of someone caught up in a hostile environment, such as a riot or an attack on an African village. My impression was that he was a missionary. He fell during the fracas, and someone stepped on his glasses, and I noticed that one of the lenses was broken. I prayed for protection for him.

One Sunday morning prior to going to church, I was in the kitchen and felt a prodding from the Lord to pray for my son Micah, and surfing came to mind. I prayed for his safety. I called him that afternoon and invited him over to watch the Super Bowl game. I asked him if he went surfing that morning. He said yes and said that it was very short. He said he paddled out into very high waves and was contemplating whether he should try them or not. He said to himself, *I really don't have to do this,* decided not to try the waves, paddled to shore, and went home.

While on a cruise that included Istanbul, Turkey, we left the Aegean Sea, and entered the Dardanelles and Sea of Marmara, I saw many villages and cities with towering mosques. As we passed each site, I prayed that the Lord would shine His light on that area. I did so via a modified song titled, "Shine Jesus Shine" that was written by a British singer-songwriter Graham Kendrick.

A few months later, a missionary from Greece I met for the second time mentioned that the emirs of several mosques along the route I had prayed claimed to have been visited by the Lord Jesus. Was it my prayers that caused it? I really won't know until I'm called up yonder.

During a Saturday morning prayer session, I received a vision following a discussion about prayer.

> **Vision Concerning the World**
> **When**: Saturday morning men's prayer group, February 25, 2006
> **Where**: Faith Chapel
> **Background**: A discussion had taken place concerning prayer. We discussed that there seemed to be a greater focus on prayer during crisis situations such as 9/11 or when the failed moon mission almost cost the lives of the astronauts returning to earth.
> **Description**: I saw a dark purple sphere being held by a white hand. The white hand became more predominant. Then I saw a vertical string of similar objects. They were brown, evenly spaced,

and in the shape of gourds. Then I saw an upside down insignia of an army private. It was in the shape of the letter V. Then I saw two golden keys on a key ring.

Interpretation:

> Dark purple—Darkness was upon the face of the earth.
> White hand—The earth is in the hand of the Lord.
> Vertical string—Explosive line charges, where the explosions take place sequentially along the line in a timed fashion so that each explosion adds to the next explosion. Probably means that one disaster will occur after the next, adding to the devastation of the previous events.
> Army insignia—The V stands for victory. The Lord's army will have victory over the enemy.
> Two golden keys—The Lord holds the keys to Hades and death (Rev. 1:18).

Summary: Darkness is on the face of the earth. However, the earth is in the hand of the Lord. Disasters will multiply, but the Lord's army will have victory over the enemy, for the Lord holds the keys to Hades and death.

The takeaway from this vision is that although prayer intensifies during a major crisis, it does not necessarily mean that peace will be the end product. Christians need to trust the Lord and allow His plan to be fulfilled.

The vision also demonstrates that an interpretation is subject to the prophet. Very, very few people know what an explosive line array is. The Spirit knew I had knowledge of such a device and that He could use the knowledge to effectively communicate with me.

Some visions are seen during a time of music, singing, and lifting up of hands to the Lord. The more tranquil the sound, the easier it is to meditate and receive a word from the Lord. Loud or distorted music seems to quench the Spirit.

I have felt the Spirit in a very strong way during worship and have danced before the Lord at times. I find this to be more acceptable in the nondenominational charismatic circles. I'm not convinced that I've felt the Spirit as strong as my dad did when I was young, but I probably have come close to it at times.

Experience has taught me that praying with a group of sincere Christians draws the Holy Spirit in a powerful way. This allows for the gifts of the Spirit to flow, whether in visions, healings, counseling, or driving out unclean spirits.

CHAPTER 8

A Message to God's People

The following visions appear directed toward the congregation or God's people in general:

Vision of the Water and Wine
When: March 28, 1988, early morning prayer
Where: MBCF
Description: I saw a wine glass/goblet. At first it was empty. Then it had water in it. The water changed to wine. Then it became empty again. An unfolded rose appeared in the goblet. A satellite antenna appeared. Then I saw a partially unfolded rose, which was followed by a broken glass. Then I saw a daisy (flower with a brown center and yellow petals).
Interpretation:

> Empty wine glass—emptiness, unbeliever
> Wine glass with water—decision to follow Christ, repentance

Water changing to wine—receiving the Word of God
Glass empty—lack of instruction
Unfolded rose—a new beginning
Satellite antenna—receive instruction
Partially unfolded rose—growing in the Word
Broken glass—denying yourself
Daisy—final product of perfection

Summary: Before you made a decision for Christ, you were empty and lacked instruction. When you decided to repent and follow Jesus, you became a new creation in Christ. As you receive instruction, you will grow in Christ. Deny yourself and move on to perfection.

Comment: It is interesting to see how the Spirit aided the interpretation by repeating the sequence; emptiness becomes lack of instruction, a decision to follow Christ becomes an unfolded rose, and receiving the Word of God becomes receive instruction.

Vision of the Handicap Logo
When: June 7, 1988, early morning prayer
Where: MBCF
Background: The prayer leader sought improvement in the prayer approach. One of the suggestions was to set aside some time to allow the Lord to speak to us.
Description: I saw a handicap logo. Then I saw a bicycle. Then I saw a tricycle.

Interpretation:

> Handicap logo—One-way communication leaves you handicapped.
> Bicycle—Two-way communication allows you to ride a bicycle.
> Tricycle—As children, you are riding tricycles.

Summary: It is the desire of our Lord to speak to us. Part of His love for us is that He gives us instructions and guidance. If we don't receive these instructions, how are we to grow and develop? One-way communication leaves us handicapped. We are children who need instruction. We are riding tricycles. We need to let the Lord teach us to ride bicycles.

Comment: The Spirit of the Lord came upon me in a powerful way when the leader set aside a couple of minutes for the Lord. I believe the Lord was very pleased with this change.

Vision of the Canoe
When: Early morning, September 20, 1988
Where: MBCF
Background: I'm not sure what the issue between them was, but a lady wanted prayer for her husband.
Description: I saw a canoe. Then I saw a flashlight. A thumb appeared with the focus on the thumb nail. This was followed by two hands

holding a sheet of paper. Then I saw a glass tube or pipe.

Interpretation:

> Canoe—I am He who moves upon the face of the waters.
> Flashlight—I am the light of the world.
> Thumb—I am He who was nailed to the cross.
> Two hands holding a sheet of paper—Read the Word of God.
> Pipe—Let My spirit flow through you.

Summary: The above interpretation is self-evident.

Comment: Although this prophecy was for an individual, it belongs in the same category as speaking to the congregation. When people have issues or problems, the solutions are found in the Word and through prayer.

Vision of the Bottles

When: Early morning, October 5, 1988

Where: MBCF

Description: I saw a microphone. Then I saw a mixer followed by a microscope. Then I saw crystal-clear bottles lined up, one behind the other.

Interpretation:

> Microphone—Speak to the congregation.
> Mixer—Stir them up.

Microscope—Used to examine small things.

Crystal-clear bottles—Holy and clean bodies

Summary: Speak to the congregation. Stir them up. Exhort them to examine themselves, even in the smallest of things. Tell them to clean out their vessels and present them holy and clean before the Lord.

Comment: Rob Wheeler spoke at a church service a few days earlier, and one of his statements was to root out the evil nature within ourselves and prepare for the Day of Atonement. This vision appears to confirm his message.

Vision of the Woven Basket
When: October 30, 1988, during evening church service
Where: MBCF
Description: I saw a woven basket followed by wheat bound in a circle. The wheat transitioned to candlesticks with light bulbs on top. This transitioned to hollow candles and then transitioned to empty soda bottles on an assembly line to be filled. I asked the Lord if there was any more, and then I saw a telephone receiver and ice cream sugar cone and then an ice cream cone with ice cream on top. It ended with someone drinking a bottle of soda.
Interpretation:

Woven basket—gathering

Wheat bound in a circle—sons of the kingdom
Candlesticks with light bulbs—bride of Christ
Hollow candlesticks—foolish virgins
Empty soda bottles—no oil, need to be filled with the Spirit
Telephone—I am calling My bride.
Sugar cone and ice cream—land of milk and honey
Drinking a bottle of soda—drink My sweet wine.

Summary: I am coming to gather My bride. Do not be like the foolish virgins whose lamps lacked oil. I am calling My bride to enter the land of milk and honey and drink of My sweet wine.

Vision Concerning Distractions
When: April 21, 2007, during a small group huddle
Where: Faith Chapel
Background: The leader opened up with coming into the room and trying to read his Bible while being distracted by a cell phone call and everyone around talking and someone tossing a soft baseball at him. The point he was making was that we tend to get so distracted with the world around us that we don't take the time to focus on things of the Lord.
Description: I saw the following: a current measuring device, a magnifying glass, a skunk,

a *Star Trek* ship like the *Enterprise*, and a pair of scissors.

Interpretation:

> Current measuring device—a device that you clamp around a wire to measure the current. Probably measuring current events or activities or what one is doing currently.
> Magnifying glass—focusing on or examining in detail what is taking place.
> Skunk—apparently what the Lord measures and sees stinks
> *Star Trek* ship—be enterprising and separate yourself from the world
> Scissors—cut out
> Next image—There was none. I seemed to be distracted by the noise that the children were making in the room next door. No matter how much I tried to focus on getting the rest of the vision, it did not appear. Then it finally dawned on me. The Lord was saying, "Cut out the distractions."

Summary: The Lord is measuring and examining our activities. He is not pleased with our worldliness. He wants us to separate ourselves from this. He wants us to cut out worldly distractions.

Dream about a Baseball Game
When: January 27, 1994

Description: The scene was a baseball field. Our team was not doing well. They were not taking the game seriously. A female batter hit a solid line drive to the outfield, and the players didn't hustle to get it. I was trying to play the game correctly. The ball that went into the outfield changed to three different colored balls, and the outfielder dragged the three balls by a string toward the infield. The person dragging the balls was planning a trip to Canada before going home. His interest was in Canada rather than on the game.

Interpretation: The contest between good and evil is not being played well by the church. The whore of Babylon is attacking Christianity with great strength. Christianity is dragging the name of the Father, Son, and Holy Spirit in the dirt. Worldly interests are distracting Christians from having victory over the enemy.

Vision of a Fighter Aircraft
When: May 17, 2008, during a small group huddle
Where: Faith Chapel
Description: The scene was in black and white. The silhouette of a fighter aircraft (similar to a P-51) approached me as it flew close to a dark ocean. The words "fight the good fight" came to mind. Then I saw a sea plane flying very close to the ocean. Then I saw a Chinook helicopter close to the water and another one in the background. A nuclear submarine appeared on the surface of the water. Then I saw a hovercraft, like the

modern ones that land marines on the shore in a battle. A pair of glasses appeared. Then I saw an ice cream cone with a very tall swirl of white and chocolate ice cream. There was a definite distinction between the colors from bottom to top: white, chocolate, white, chocolate, white, chocolate, etc. Then I saw a clear plastic cup filled with a chocolate drink with a straw in it.

Interpretation:

> Fighter aircraft—Fight the good fight.
> Dark ocean—Darkness is on the face of the world.
> Sea plane—Darkness on the face of the deep can be plainly seen.
> Helicopter—Mankind needs to be rescued from the sea of darkness.
> Two helicopters—This can be accomplished by bearing witness of the knowledge and understanding of the ways of God.
> Submarine—Put on the armor of God as you enter the world.
> Hovercraft—The Spirit is hovering over the face of the waters.
> Glasses—The Spirit sees the outward workings of the world.
> Ice cream cone with white and chocolate swirls—a great mixture of Christianity and the world.
> Cup of chocolate drink and straw—Do not drink of the cup of the world.

Summary: Fight the good fight, for darkness can be plainly seen on the face of the deep. Mankind needs to be rescued from the sea of darkness. Knowledge and understanding of God's ways need to be made known. Put on the armor of God as you enter the world. The Spirit is hovering over the face of the waters and sees the outward workings of the world. There is a great mixture of Christianity and the world. Do not drink the cup of the world.

The earth was without form, and void; and darkness was on the face of the deep. And the Spirit of God was hovering over the face of the waters (Gen. 1:2).

For My people are foolish, They have not known Me. They are silly children, and they have no understanding. They are wise to do evil, But to do good they have no knowledge. I beheld the earth, and indeed it was without form, and void; and the heavens, they had no light (Jer. 4:22–23).

Vision of the Cluster of Gems
When: January 17, 2011
Where: On the *Spirit*, a Carnival cruise ship
Background: About a week or so earlier, I was seeking a word for the year 2011.
Description: I saw a dense cluster of small gems (they sparkled like diamonds). I could see the different colors reflecting off the many facets. Then I saw a kerosene lantern. It did not appear

to be lit. Then I saw what appeared to be a very dark green globe (or a black globe with a tinge of green in it). The globe was suspended over a smooth, stained piece of wood. One side of the wood served as the base, and the other side angled up to hold the globe.

Interpretation:

> Dense cluster of gems—the multifaceted nature of God
> Unlit lamp—The light is not shining.
> Dark globe—Darkness is on the face of the earth.
> Ting of green—There is little righteousness.
> Wooden stand—sins of humanity
> Globe suspended in wooden stand—earth suspended in sin

Comment: This interpretation brings to mind the two verses quoted above. This vision indicates how the earth is viewed by the Spirit at this present time. However, Genesis 1 continues with the following verse:

Then God said, "Let there be light"; and there was light (Gen. 1:3).

I suspect that the Lord is saying that during the darkness of this age, His multi-dimensional nature will shine forth. Perhaps the latter rain will begin to fall and there will be a mighty outpouring of the Spirit. This may explain the following dream.

Dream about Wheat
When: February 8, 2002
Where: Home
Description: I was watching grain (wheat) falling from a combine. The scene appeared to be in the Midwest. After watching the grain fall for a while, I saw a rifle with a scope fall out of the combine along with the grain.
Interpretation: The grain represents the Word of God. An abundance of God's Word will be poured out. The rifle with scope says that the enemy will be slain by the Word of God.

In summary, the basic message to God's people is that they should clean out their vessels and fill them with the Spirit. The Lord desires that people remove sin from their lives, listen to the Lord, and be as wise virgins. In the latter days, the latter rain will be greater than the former rain (i.e., there will be a greater outpouring of the Holy Spirit in the latter days, far exceeding the pouring out in the early days of Christianity). The light will shine brightly.

CHAPTER 9

Proverbs

An interesting analysis would be to connect a few visions and see if they follow a similar pattern found in the book of Proverbs. First, each of the visions will be listed with their respective titles, descriptions, and interpretations. Then the interpretations will be listed in chronological order.

Vision of the Lion
Where: Home, family room
When: October 1996
Description: I saw the following: a lion (the word *courage* came to mind), comb, a brush facing up with the focus on the bristles, a clip (comb type), an aimed rifle, one of the Marx brothers (Harpo), and another Marx brother (Chico).
Interpretation:

> Lion—lion of the tribe of Judah
> Comb—used for grooming
> Brush facing up—brush up

Hair clip—take hold of what you have
Two Marx brothers—marksmen

Summary: Have courage like a lion. Prepare yourself. Brush up on your learning. Take hold of what you have. Become skillful at hitting your target like a marksman.

Vision of the Sea Anemone
Where: Home
When: November 1996
Description: I saw the following: a sea anemone opening and closing its mouth, a hand appeared as part of the anemone, and a skull viewed from several angles. The skull appeared marked, showing part of the skull or areas of the skull.
Interpretation: See the working hand of the enemy upon various sections of the mind.

Vision of Power
Where: June Lake condo
When: May 1999
Background: Group praise and worship
Description: I saw two chain link fences joined by a narrow gate. On the other side of the gate was a long, straight, narrow blacktop road with trees on each side. The next scene was of a power pole with an electric meter on it and a couple of wires coming from it. The next scene was of a vessel in the shape of a blender being filled.
Interpretation: The two fences are two witnesses (knowledge and understanding) that guide people

to the narrow gate. Upon entering the narrow gate, they are to follow the straight and narrow road. Upon doing so, power will be meted out to them, and their vessels will be filled with the fruit of the Spirit.

Vision of the River
Where: June Lake condo
When: May 1999
Background: Praying for healing for someone's back
Description: I saw a river. It was bright, white (like that of a reflection off water seen on a cloudy day), and flowing down a mountain. The words, "There's a river of life flowing out of me" came to mind.
Interpretation: There's a river of life flowing out of me.

Vision of the Stream
Where: June Lake condo
When: May 1999
Background: Praying for healing of someone's back (a very humble, old gentleman, strong in the Lord)
Description: I saw a clear stream of water in a forest flowing over a small waterfall. The word "peace" came to mind.
Interpretation: Be at peace, for in Me there is peace.

Vision of the Face of a Lion
Where: Faith Chapel
When: February 2001
Background: I was praying and seeking the Lord while meditating upon Colossians 1:9, "For this reason we also, since the day; we heard it, do not cease to pray for you, and to ask that you may be filled with the knowledge of His will in all wisdom and spiritual understanding."
Description: I saw the following: the face of a lion (the expression "lion of the tribe of Judah" came to mind), then a two-story old New England style house, the same house with a steeple on it, and the face of a lion up close enough where I could see the individual hairs on his nose.
Interpretation:

> Lion—Jesus, power, strength, boldness, Lion of the tribe of Judah
> Two-story old New England style house with a steeple
> > Two—number of witnesses, knowledge and understanding
> > House—mature Christian
> Lion up close—boldness

Summary: I am the Lion of the tribe of Judah. As a mature Christian, bear witness of My knowledge and understanding of the ways of God with boldness.

Comment: During a dream within a week prior to the vision, I received a message to go forth with boldness.

Vision of the Ears
Where: Faith Chapel
When: September 3, 2005, during Saturday morning prayer meeting
Background: Several people were discussing the flooding in New Orleans.
Description: At the beginning of the prayer meeting, during worship, I saw an ear on the right side of someone's head. It was a normal-looking ear. While praying over people who were sitting in the chair, I saw an ear on the left side of someone's head, and it appeared pointed, like that of a leprechaun.
Interpretation: For the interpretation, three verses came to mind:

> He that has an ear, let him hear what the Spirit is saying to the churches (Rev. 2:7).

> And He will set the sheep on His right hand, but the goats on the left (Matt. 25:33).

> My sheep hear My voice ... (John 10:27).

> The ear on the right—The sheep will hear what the Holy Spirit is saying.
> The leprechaun-looking ear—The goats will hear what the spirit of the world is saying.

Vision of the Wine Glass
Where: Faith Chapel
When: March 4, 2006, Saturday morning men's prayer group
Description: During worship I saw a wine glass being held by a hand. Both the wine glass and the hand had a white, ghostly look. The wine glass changed shape and became more elegant looking (a design I was familiar with). During prayer, the same vision appeared. The difference was that the hand with the glass was moving in such a way as to suggest, "Come here." Then a knight's helmet appeared.
Interpretation:

> Hand—hand of the Lord
> Wine glass—Word of God
> Change in wine glass shape—elegant, good
> Hand and glass moving—beckoning
> Knight's helmet—helmet of salvation

Summary: The Savior invites you to drink of His most excellent wine, the Word of God.
Comment: This vision reminded me of our small group meeting on Wednesday when we studied the first part of John 2 (the wedding in Cana). The motion of beckoning seems to imply an invitation. I puzzled over this interpretation for quite some time. I wasn't sure if the Holy Spirit was encouraging me to invite someone in the group to receive the message of salvation or

encouraging the group as a whole to hear or read the Word of God.

Taking the above interpretations and putting them in chronological order results in the following:

> Have courage like a lion. Prepare yourself. Brush up on your learning. Take hold of what you have. Become skillful at hitting your target like a marksman. See the working hand of the enemy upon various sections of the mind. Knowledge and understanding will serve to guide you to the narrow gate. Enter the narrow gate and follow the straight and narrow road. You will receive power, and you will be filled with the fruit of the Spirit. There's a river of life flowing out of Me. In Me you will find peace. I am the Lion of the tribe of Judah. As a mature Christian, bear witness of knowledge and understanding of the ways of God with boldness. The sheep will hear what the Holy Spirit is saying. The goats will hear what the spirit of the world is saying. The Savior invites you to drink of His most excellent wine, the Word of God.

Given the approach of receiving visions, interpreting them, and then putting them in chronological order, it's not too difficult to believe that prophets of old could have used this method to write the Psalms and Proverbs. The prophecies would most likely be more cohesive, as there would not be such a time difference between visions as those shown above.

CHAPTER 10

PROPHECIES TO INDIVIDUALS

Many times the Lord will stir me to provide advice or comfort to others through visions. The following visions were received at various meetings, such as prayer groups, small group meetings, retreats, and during church services.

Vision of a Hoist
When: August 18, 1988, during early morning prayer
Where: MBCF
Background: As I passed by a prayer group member, I overheard her requesting a comforting word just to know that God is still with her. I prayed and asked for a word concerning her request.
Description: I saw a hoist and then a set of tongs. The phrase that came to mind was, "Fear not, for I am with you, and I will not let you go."

Interpretation:

> Hoist—command to go and lift her up
> Tongs—Tell her that I'm holding her in the palm of My hands.

Comment: The message to her was, "The Lord is holding you in the palm of His hands. Fear not, for I am with you, and I will not let you go." This message really lifted her spirit.

Vision of a Boot
When: October 18, 1988, during early morning prayer
Where: MBCF
Background: I dreamed a dream, and in my spirit, I thought it was a message for someone. During morning prayer, I asked the Lord who the dream was for, and I received the following vision.
Description: I saw a sea captain on a ship. He was looking through binoculars. The outer lenses of the binoculars were black with eyes in the center. Then I saw a car from the early fifties. Then I saw someone's lower leg wearing blue jeans and a brown leather work boot.
Interpretation:

> Captain—I am the Captain of Hosts.
> Binoculars—I search to and fro upon the earth.

Eyes in dark background—I see into dark places.

Car from the early fifties—I'm not sure what this means; perhaps when the person was born (which means the person was in his or her mid-thirties).

Blue jeans and boot—a description of the person to whom the dream applies

Comment: As I raised my head and opened my eyes, I saw a member of the prayer team who had entered the room after I had closed my eyes and began to pray. He wore the same color blue jeans and brown leather work boots as seen in the vision. I was certain that he was the one with whom I was to share the dream. Incidentally, he was in his mid-thirties.

Vision Concerning the Heart
When: December 26, 1989, during evening worship with some friends
Where: Home
Description: I saw a chain and padlock and then a heart-shaped mirror. This was followed by an opening red book.
Interpretation:

Chain and padlock—bound
Heart-shaped mirror—examine your heart
Opening red book—Open your heart to others.

Summary: You keep your heart under lock and key. Examine your heart, and open it up to others.

Vision of the Gavel
When: January 5, 1997, evening healing service
Where: A church in the San Diego Area
Background: A known healer was praying for finances for everyone and in particular for my friend.
Description: I saw a gavel that was resting upright (as if judgment had been made). Then I saw a peaceful scene of a lagoon. The water was very, very slightly choppy. It was not daylight but perhaps a half hour or so after sunset.
Interpretation:

> Upright gavel—Judgment has been made.
> Peaceful scene—Be at peace concerning this issue. Lay it to rest.

Comment: My friend had lost a lot of money in a business venture and was praying to get it back. The interpretation seems to indicate that for whatever reason, judgment had been made and that he wasn't to expect any recovery. He was to be at peace over the issue and put it behind him. It is not an answer people like to hear when praying for a miracle.

Vision of the Black-Eyed Susan
When: April 22, 2001, during evening service

Where: Faith Chapel
Description: I saw a woman holding the world over her head. She was wearing a red top (sweater, jacket?). Then I saw a flower with yellow petals and a brown center (Black-Eyed Susan). A crystal-clear glass appeared. Then I saw the flower next to the glass. Then I saw the flower in the glass. Then a crystal-clear glass teapot appeared.
Interpretation:

> Woman holding the world—She holds the world in her hands.
> Flower—brings happiness
> Glass—her vessel or body
> Glass with flower—She needs to be filled with happiness.
> Glass teapot—contains the Spirit, a source of happiness

Summary: You hold the world in your hands, and you are not happy. You need to add happiness to your life. The true source of happiness is the Holy Spirit. Invite Him into your life.
Comment: It turns out that my friend's wife was sitting next to me, and she was wearing a red jacket. My friend had just passed away. I shared the vision with her, as I was certain that it was for her. She was very grateful to receive the message.

I have had several visions focused on exhorting people not to drink beer. The following vision is interesting because I saw it twice. I seldom see a vision repeat itself.

Vision of the Mug of Beer

When: September 29, 2001, during Saturday morning prayer

Where: Faith Chapel

Background: Seen during the time of worship

Description: I saw a mug of beer with suds on top and around the bottom as well. I saw this vision twice.

Comment: When receiving a vision twice, it usually means that it is very, very important to get the word out. I believe the message was for one or more people in the prayer meeting. It basically was saying to stop excessive beer drinking. One of my close friends mentioned after the meeting that he had a drinking problem and that he had gone five days without taking a drink.

Vision of the Wooden Barrels

When: October 6, 2001, during Saturday morning prayer.

Where: Faith Chapel

Description: During prayer and worship, I saw a wooden barrel, and under the barrel I saw a white X. In the next scene, I saw several ramps in a row with a wooden barrel at the bottom of each ramp. The vision seemed to focus on the black Xs on the barrels. The impression was that the barrels were full of an alcoholic beverage of some kind, perhaps beer, ale, or whisky.

Interpretation: The one barrel with the white X contained the fruit of the Spirit. The barrels with the black X contained alcohol or fruit of the world. The Spirit seemed to be saying, "Drink of the fruit of the Spirit. Do not drink alcoholic beverages."

And do not be drunk with wine, in which is dissipation; but be filled with the Spirit (Eph. 5:18).

Comment: The vision seemed to be a follow up from the previous week's vision on the mug of beer. I believe the Lord is telling His people to avoid drinking alcoholic beverages.

Vision of the Doors
When: May 8, 2003
Where: June Lake, during evening fellowship
Background: I asked the Lord how I might serve Him in a significant way.
Description: I saw many doors, one behind the other. The impression was that these doors had to be closed. Then I saw one door. It was closed. The vision focused on the doorknob.
Interpretation: Many doors had to be closed, one at a time, before opening the one door.

Vision of the Rooster on a Housetop
When: October 30, 2004
Where: Home
Background: I awoke early and decided to sleep awhile longer before getting up and heading out for the Saturday morning men's prayer meeting. I asked the Lord to wake me in time to make it

to men's prayer. I awoke at 6:02 a.m. The time was perfect, as it gave me enough time to shower and call my parents before heading out. As I sat on the edge of the bed shortly after waking, the Lord gave me a vision of a rooster on the roof of a house.

Interpretation: That was your wakeup call from on high (the rooster was high up on the rooftop).

Comment: I believe the Lord was saying, "You asked Me to wake you. Aren't you going to thank Me?" I immediately thanked the Lord. The vision brought a smile to my face. There have been many times when I have asked the Lord to wake me at a specific time, and He has been most excellent to comply.

Vision of the Valve
When: February 18, 2006, Saturday morning at men's prayer.
Where: Faith Chapel
Background: The men were praying.
Description: I saw a pipe valve, the kind that you find on a large pipe.
Interpretation: It probably meant that someone in the group might have a problem with a heart valve. It seems that someone in the last week or so mentioned he or she had a heart valve problem, but I couldn't recall who it was.
Comment: I mentioned the vision during the meeting. It turns out that the individual who was sitting next to me had a problem with a

leaky heart valve. Incidentally, in all my years of attending Saturday morning prayer, he never sat next to me. Also, during breakfast that morning, he and another prayer member were sitting across from me. The other prayer member mentioned that he had a heart valve problem as well. I prayed over the first person at church and prayed for each of them during the following week.

Vision of the Log
When: March 11, 2006, Saturday morning men's prayer group meeting
Where: Faith Chapel
Description: During worship, I saw a raft or barge with a large log on it. There were several cables bunched together to hold the log on the craft. The log was definitely well secured on the craft. The next scene was of a wilderness with many tall evergreen trees with a river running through it and mountains in the background and a meadow across the river with deer. The sky was thickly overcast, with puffs of clouds in the background; it was something like a cold, damp, windy northwest scene. The river was running wild, with white caps along the length of it.
Interpretation:

> Raft or barge—an individual
> Large log—major sin
> Cable holding the log in place—holding on to a major sinful nature

Wilderness scene—Holding on to the sinful nature will result in a long, unpleasant, rough ride in the wilderness.

Comment: I'm not sure who this was for, but it was a good word for anyone who can identify with this vision.

Vision of the Power Cord
When: June 9, 2007, during Saturday morning men's prayer meeting
Where: Faith Chapel
Background: I prayed on the way to the prayer meeting that the Lord's power would be seen during the meeting.
Description: During worship, I saw the plug of a power cord. It was a three-pronged plug. The vision focused on the plug.
Interpretation: It seems that to receive power, one needs to connect with the Lord.

Vision of the Sunflower
When: August 25, 2007, morning small group leadership meeting
Where: Faith Chapel
Description: I saw the following series of objects/events: a croquet mallet, a hand writing with a pen, the pen being dropped forward with the hand opening, a palm tree, a sunflower (yellow petals with brown center; the center of the sunflower had an opening in the shape of an eye with words and symbols running from right to left), a pineapple,

a Kool-Aid pitcher with a smiley face, a glass container with red liquid at the bottom, two paths that were parallel and of the same length and in the shape of popsicle sticks, and six stars arranged with three stars over each path.

Interpretation:

> Croquet mallet—A croquet mallet hits a wooden ball in the direction of a goal. The Lord is moving me in a certain direction with a goal in mind.
> Hand writing with a pen—This is what I write to you.
> Pen dropping with hand open—And this is what I am about to say.
> Palm tree—I hold you in the palm of My hand.
> Sunflower—Son, "Behold My Son"
> Center of sunflower with words and symbols—I will speak to you in words and symbols through my Son.
> Pineapple—You are the apple of my eye who pines after Me.
> Kool-aid pitcher with smiley face—I will quench your thirst for My Word with pleasure.
> Glass container with red liquid—Come, drink of my wine.
> Two straight, parallel paths of the same length—I will provide you with an equal amount of knowledge and understanding of My ways. As it says in Proverbs 2:6, "For the

Lord gives wisdom; out of His mouth come knowledge and understanding."

Six stars—Six is the number of man.

Three stars—Three is the number for the Father, Son, and Holy Spirit.

Summary: I am moving you in a certain direction with a goal in mind. This is what I write to you, and this is what I am about to say. I hold you in the palm of My hand. Behold My Son. I will speak to you in words and symbols through my Son. You are the apple of My eye who pines after Me. I will quench your thirst for My Word with pleasure. Come, drink of My wine. I will provide you with an equal amount of knowledge and understanding of My ways. In regard to the knowledge and understanding that I have provided to you, I exhort you to minister to the world in the name of the Father, Son, and Holy Spirit.

Comment: As an anecdote, just prior to writing the vision down for this book, I went outside to praise God and ask Him if writing this book was His will for me. I needed some encouragement to continue this effort. Upon returning to the computer and writing the vision, I realized that His answer was in the vision. The Lord knew ahead of time that I needed encouragement and probably prodded me to take a break before continuing with this chapter. It brought a smile to my face knowing that the Lord is at my side.

Vision of the Fruit of the Spirit
When: October 5, 2007, during small group coaches meeting
Where: Leader's house
Background: Not exactly sure, but I had the feeling that the leader and his wife may have been discussing his role as a leader of the small groups.
Description: I saw crystal-clear water glasses close together in a row with the focus on two of them. I'm not sure what the next object was. It looked like a candle or lamp base tipped over. The base was the color of the chair across from me. A watch with a square face appeared on a flat cushion (the color and design of the cloth on the chair opposite of me). The vision focused in on the watch three times. There was a horizontal vase with clear liquid pouring out of it. A variety of fruit appeared in the liquid flowing out.
Interpretation:

> Crystal water glasses—members of the small group coaches team
> Two glasses—the leader and his wife
> Watch on the seat—It is time to sit and relax.
> Focus on the watch three times—It is time. It is time. It is time.
> Vase and fruit—fruit of the Spirit

Summary: To the leader and his wife, it is time to sit and relax. It is time. It is time. It is time to be filled with the fruit of the Spirit.

Comment: While the leader was speaking, I asked the Lord to confirm the interpretation of the vision by having the leader mention the fruit of the Spirit. Immediately, the leader began to talk about the fruit of the Spirit. I felt the presence of the Spirit for quite some time during the meeting. At one point the Spirit was so strong that tears came to my eyes. I suspect the Lord was saying that it was time for the leader and his wife to step down from the position and to relax and focus on being filled with the Spirit.

Vision in the Tunnel
When: March 6, 2009, during a small groups coaches meeting
Where: leader's home
Description: I saw the top view of a palm tree with four green leaves. Then I saw a purple flower (the word "iris" came to mind). The vision focused on the brown center of the flower. Then I saw the aft end of a jet engine. Then I saw the aft end of a jet engine again. Then I saw a single-engine plane. It was flying in the clouds. The background was yellow and brown. A spinning black-and-white-striped vortex appeared. It transitioned to going down a tunnel with the black and white sides spinning. A bright light appeared at the end of the tunnel. Several black arms (they looked like rubber gloves) stretched toward the light. A white arm with the same shape stretched out from the light and placed several dark nuggets (black with brown tinges to it, about twenty or so) in

the palm of a hand. I looked closely at the nuggets or stones and was questioning the value of the objects. Then, the side of the palm turned a bright yellow-white, and I saw the skull of a dinosaur. Immediately the hand turned the same color, and in the hand were perhaps hundreds of opaque, yellow-white rough gems (perhaps diamonds in the rough).

Interpretation:

> Palm tree and leaves—I have you in the palm of my hand. I am your covering.
> Purple iris with focus on brown center—I looked up a picture of an iris, and indeed, the image that I saw was an iris. Iris means "rainbow" in Greek. It is also the colored part around the pupil of the eye. Perhaps the Lord is saying, "You are the flower of My eye" (purple being the symbol of royalty).
> Aft end of jet engine—Thrust (being shown twice means that it will happen very soon). Probably means something will be forced forward in the near future.
> Airplane in clouds—You shall fly with me in the clouds.
> Black-and-white, spinning tunnel, bright light—In a trance approaching heaven.
> Black arms—unworthy hands reaching out for a gift from God
> White arm—the hand of God providing a gift
> Dark nuggets—coal

Dinosaur skull—a long time has passed
Gems—diamonds

Summary: I have you in the palm of your hand. I am your covering. You are the flower of my eye. I will thrust you forward in a short period of time, and you will fly aloft with Me. The gift given to you while you are in darkness may not seem valuable at the time. As coal is turned into diamonds over a long period of time, so too will the gift given to you during pressure and time turn into something of great value.

Comment: If this vision is for me, I wonder if it is a reflection of my gift of visions and that the gift will eventually bear fruit. The vision could also have been for someone else in the group.

Dream about Highways
When: July 22, 1990
Description: I had a choice between two highways to travel on. I wasn't certain as to which highway to take. I may have been confused as to even where I was going. The two highways were numbered seven and thirteen. The one labeled thirteen was dark and gloomy. The other was wide and open.
Interpretation: When the future is uncertain, do not take the path of darkness. Take the road that is wide and open.

Dream about the White Horse
When: March 18, 1997

Description: A beautiful white horse appeared. The hair on the horse was thick and a few inches longer than that of a normal horse. Jesus was near my side. When the horse ran, it ran swiftly as if there was no weight from the horse on the ground. It appeared that I had an opportunity to ride the horse. The thought of any weight on the horse caused the horse to look at me in a perturbed manner.

Interpretation: The white horse will effectively carry you into battle when your faith is made full and you rid yourself of the weight of the world. He who sat on the white horse in Revelation 19:11 was called Faithful and True, and His name is called "the Word of God." In righteousness He judges and wages war.

Vision Concerning the Writing of this Book
When: June 19, 2010
Where: Home, Tucson, AZ
Background: I asked the Lord to reveal to me in a clear way what my next project should be. I was trying to choose between: 1) working on my nuclear physics paper, 2) writing about my experiences with the gift of visions and dreams, 3) working on both, or 4) working on none of these.
Description: I clearly saw the number two underlined in red.
Comment: This indicated that he Lord wanted me to write a book about my experiences with visions and dreams.

Vision of the Golden Cup

When: February 28, 1989, during evening service and during communion prayer

Where: MBCF

Background: A lady gave a performance that involved enacting a Christian message (a prophecy, if I correctly recall). I didn't write down or remember the details of the performance, but I do remember it was impressive. The following vision occurred after the performance.

Description: I saw a large, beautiful golden cup with handles on each side like that of a first place trophy. A purple cloth (bright fine linen) was draped over each handle and met at the base.

Interpretation: The gold stood for divinity, and the purple robe stood for royalty (king). This trophy indicated that the Lord was exceedingly pleased with her performance. There could be a double meaning, as the vision occurred during the communion prayer. It could be an invitation to drink of the Lord's cup.

Comment: My wife told me that the lady was quite nervous before the performance. I shared the vision with the lady, and she appeared to be quite pleased to hear what I had to say.

In summary, the dominant messages to individuals seem to be centered on lifting people up. Just letting people know that the Lord is listening is enough to lift their spirits and increase faith. Jesus is the Prince of Peace. He wants peace in our lives. Messages to individuals are designed to remove turmoil and replace it with a spirit of peace.

For example, if drinking beer creates issues, then cutting out alcohol will remove those issues. It is better to be filled with the Spirit, who will bring comfort and peace into our lives.

CHAPTER 11

TO CHURCH LEADERS

Early on, I had a number of visions that served as warnings to church leaders. As it turns out, my first recorded vision addressed a warning to those who misused church funds. The following vision was received during prayer:

Vision of the Candle
When: April 4, 1988, during morning prayer
Where: MBCF
Background: Prior to the prayer, there was a discussion about two televangelists who were indicted for misappropriating donor funds.
Description: I saw wax on a flat surface. A wick and a flame appeared in the center. Then a candle grew up out of the center. It was tall and slender. All of a sudden, the flame was blown out. The end of the wick was as red as an ember, and smoke drifted away from it. The next scene showed a row of unlit candles chained together in bondage.

(I got the impression they were moving in unison in a dark and dreary atmosphere.)

Interpretation: The candle is someone who has grown tall in the ministry. For some reason, perhaps because he or she misrepresented the ministry, the Lord has extinguished the light. Those whose flames have been extinguished are under the bondage of Satan.

Comment: Sometime after this vision, I was watching the television news and saw one of the evangelists being led from the courthouse in chains. I thought back on the vision, and said to myself, "Wow! That was prophetic."

The above vision occurred on the April 4, 1988. I experienced two dreams concerning church leadership, one on April 2 and one on April 3. The dreams were quite similar and involved the use of aircraft to represent church leaders and perhaps the organizations they represented. The two dreams are as follows:

Dream of an Airplane 1
When: April 2, 1988
Description: I spotted a long, heavy-looking military jet. It was flying slowly, as if making a landing approach. The aircraft had no wings. I marveled at the state of technology that allowed the plane to stay aloft. As it circled to make a final landing, I knew in my spirit that if the plane didn't sprout wings, it was going to crash. At this point, I was taken up and given a close view of the side of the aircraft as wings began to unfold from the body. I was on the ground again as I

watched the plane struggle to skirt over a hill to avoid crashing. After going out of view, the plane apparently circled back, and I saw it close to the ground struggling to stay aloft. There was a hole in the ground. As it neared a hill, it flipped over and the pilot tried to steer the plane over the hole upside down. The nose of the plane hit the hill at a slow speed and flipped over a house. In my spirit, the impact of the crash did not kill the pilot. As I approached the crash site, I saw a woman kneeling over two children on the ground in front of the house. One of the children tried to get up, but the mother forced him to stay down. In my spirit, I thought she was doing this to make people think her kids were injured in the accident so she could sue for damages.

Interpretation: This could be in reference to a televangelist who had his wings clipped by the churches and was given permission to fly again in one year. The wings that sprouted were the permit to fly in one year. But instead of listening to them, he decided to fly contrary (upside down) to the church's recommendations and caused his ministry to crash. Will a phoenix rise out of the ashes? How many false claims will be filed against his ministry?

The next dream occurred the following night.

Dream of an Airplane 2
When: April 3, 1988

Description: I was in the air looking down on a mountainous, desert landscape bordering the ocean. I saw a river approaching the ocean. As it approached, it appeared to be blocked by a mountain range. I expected a lake to have been formed from the blockage, but instead, the water simply disappeared. In my spirit, I was satisfied why it disappeared, but I can't recall the reason. I was taken to a place where the river ended and placed under a large aircraft that was sitting on the sand. I looked at the black tires, and the word "sins" came to mind. I felt uncomfortable, as the space between the ground and aircraft was narrowing as if the tires were sinking into the sand. I wanted out of there. I was next placed in a scene of aircraft in the desert. It had the appearance of an airplane graveyard. As I entered a nearby building, I saw scrap aluminum lying about. I handed someone some crushed aluminum cans and suspected they were worth only a few pennies.

Interpretation: The river represents the Holy Spirit. The river ends at the graveyard of planes. These planes represent fallen preachers whose sins have been exposed. The Spirit no longer flows into them. To remain under their covering is useless and risky, as they may drag you down with them. Fallen preachers are no longer filled with the Spirit and are no longer functional. They are worthless.

The following vision spoke of a warning to either the church I was attending at the time or churches in general. I list it because it presented a challenge in interpreting its symbols.

Vision of a Covering
When: February 11, 2001
Where: Evening church
Background: Worshipping and waiting on the Lord
Description: I saw a jar that contained seafood. An octopus came to mind. Then I saw a clam shell covering the seafood. A hat replaced the shell. Then I saw an octopus eye in the side of a man's head, a head like that on a coin. The head was golden in color. Then I saw another man's head that was golden in color. Then a golden bow and arrow with the string pulled back appeared. Then I saw the teeth of an alligator. This was followed by the front face of a ferocious dog or wolf showing bared teeth. The next scene was the inside of a tunnel. Thick glass lenses appeared (as from a pair of glasses). Then I saw a sheet of glass that was very bumpy, followed by drinking glasses made from the same sheet of glass. A whole bunch of buses parked next to each other appeared. Then I saw a man in southwestern gear who looked as if he was leaning into a storm. A face appeared. (I had the impression that it was Sir Isaac Newton, and I heard the expression "What goes up must come down.") Then I saw a sailing ship (perhaps of the sixteenth century) sinking bow first in a

very heavy storm. Then I saw a structure in the sea.

Interpretation:

> Jar—person
> Octopus—creature from the sea with eight tentacles, salvation
> Shell—sea creature
> Hat—covering
> Octopus eye in side of golden-colored head—Salvation is in your sight.
> Golden man—important man
> Gold bow and arrow—The Lord's weapon, conquer
> Alligator and wolf—enemy
> Thick glasses—poor vision
> Tunnel—tunnel vision
> Bricks—firm, rigid, will not move
> Tunnel—tunnel vision
> Sheet of glass—distorted view
> Drinking glass—drinking a distorted word
> Southwestern—prepare for a storm
> Isaac Newton—Those who exalt themselves will be abased.
> Sinking ship—church
> Sea—world
> Structure in the sea—a relic in the world

Summary: You are a worldly person whose covering is the world, yet you wear a hat that says, "The Lord is my covering." You are an important person who sees himself as saved. I will slay those who devour my people. You have tunnel vision. You are so rigid in your ways that you will not move. You have a distorted view of things. You quench your thirst with this distorted view. Prepare for the storm that is to come. Those who exalt themselves will be abased. Your church will sink into the sea, and it will become a byword in the world.

Comment: As if interpreting this vision wasn't challenging enough, the next challenge was to figure out to whom the vision was referring. And if I was able to figure that out (which I might have), was I the person to share this vision with that person? Now I know what the major prophets might have felt when they had to approach the priests with chastising words from the Lord. Woe is me! Woe is me!

While attending a church several times on behalf of a friend, I noticed that the majority of the members were old people. When I say old, I mean that one of the ladies walking behind me to partake in communion was one hundred years old. During an evening service at the church, I had the following vision.

Vision of the Wooden Figures
When: Sunday evening, March 15, 1998
Where: A church
Background: Pastor was praying
Description: I saw dark wooden figures sitting in the pews on both sides of the church. The wood of the figures matched the wood in the pews. The figures were thin and were all the same size and

shape. The tops of the heads of the figures came to a point. In the next scene, the church doors were open, and people began to come into the church riding bicycles. They appeared to be of a younger generation. The scene was in black and white (actually more of a gray). The next scene, also in black and white (degrees of gray), showed a few people walking a city street and maybe a cyclist as well. A newspaper was blowing on the street, and the street appeared littered but not too bad. I felt that it was a scene out of the late 1920s or early 1930s.
Interpretation:

> Wooden figures—people who have been in church so long that they are not much different than the pews they sit in. They are alive but dead.
> Young cyclists—You need to open your doors and cycle in some active young people.
> Scene from the late 1920s or early1930s—poverty

Summary: The church has a name that says it is alive, but in reality it is dead. The people are like minded and have the same point of view. They have their rituals and social activities, but they are not reaching out to the young. They need to cycle in the younger generation. They claim to be rich, yet they are poor (in spirit).
Comment: The people in and of themselves were kind and quite sociable. One of the families

befriended me and counseled me during a time when my spirit was troubled. And yes, they appeared to be upper middle class or wealthy people.

I received the following vision during prayer at a church leadership meeting.

Vision of the Drinking Glasses
When: May 26, 1994
Where: Leadership meeting at MBCF
Description: I saw two crystal-clear drinking glasses. There was a lit candle in each of them. Immediately to the left of them I saw three more crystal-clear drinking glasses. Each of them contained a lit candle. The three drinking glasses disappeared, and immediately six empty clear-crystal drinking glasses appeared and passed between the two glasses with the lit candles.
Interpretation:

> Two glasses with lit candles—two witnesses
> Three glasses with lit candles—Father, Son, and Holy Spirit
> Six empty glasses—unbelievers

Summary: The leadership of the church needs focus on bearing witness of the Word to the unsaved in the name of the Father, Son, and Holy Spirit.

Go therefore and make disciples of all the nations, baptizing them in the name of the Father and of the Son and of the Holy Spirit, teaching them to observe all things that I have commanded you; and lo, I am with you always, even to the end of the age. Amen (Matt. 8:19–20).

The following vision had a similar exhortation as the one above.

Vision of Ministry
When: April 4, 2008
Where: Small group coaches meeting at Faith Chapel
Description: I saw a reddish purple cap like a priest would wear. It had four golden, narrow bands, equally spaced, running from the top to the bottom edge. The words "royal priesthood" came to mind. The number five appeared. Then a glass container, clear as crystal, appeared. It was empty and ornate and had a triangular glass top on it. Then I saw a similar container with a square glass top on it. While meditating on these items as to what they meant, an American flag, unfolded, with its bright red, white, and blue colors suddenly appeared in front of me. It startled me. Then the red color of the flag seemed to flow into a stream of water that just appeared. The stream then appeared at a distance. It was narrow, normal in color, and flowing around a bend.

The next day at the small group huddle, the vision seemed to continue. I saw a pool of water as part of a stream. Then the same reddish purple cap seen at the beginning of the previous night's vision appeared. The words "royal priesthood" came to mind again. The cap reappeared, and the word "covering" came to mind.

Interpretation:

> Reddish purple cap—royal priesthood
> Five—ministry
> Crystalline container with triangular top—Father, Son, and Holy Spirit
> Crystalline container with square top—four corners of the earth or four directions
> Flag—stars and stripes—by My stripes you were healed, life, liberty, and the pursuit of happiness
> Red color mixing with water—Blood and water, the sacrifice that Jesus made for us
> Stream—There's life in the blood. The stream became living water of life.
> Pool of water—the gathering of those who have the water of life (small group huddle)
> Reddish cap—You are a royal priesthood, and I'm your covering.

Summary: You are a royal priesthood. Go forth and minister to the four corners of the earth in the name of the Father, Son, and Holy Spirit. By My stripes you were healed. Those who receive the message will have life, will be liberated from death, and will pursue happiness in the kingdom of God. Tell them of the sacrifice of the Son, and encourage them to drink of the water of life. You have huddled before me as a royal priesthood. I am your covering.

Vision of Church Growth
When: January 2006
Where: Home
Background: The pastor of my church mentioned that the bigger mainstream churches were not growing but instead were declining in numbers. I prayed for the church and received the following vision.
Description: I saw an empty, white five-gallon container. Then I saw a panda bear with emphasis on the black and white color. A hippopotamus with small ears appeared. The ears were wiggling to draw attention to them. Then I saw two or three variations of the head of a reptile or lizard. Then I saw a coffee can that had no label with a red clay pot inside with a dead or dehydrating green plant.
Interpretation:

> Empty, white five-gallon container—The church appears large and righteous but is empty.
> Panda bear—The church views the world in black and white.
> Hippopotamus ears—The large church listens with small ears.

> Reptile heads—In many cases, the church listens with no ears at all.
> Coffee can with no label—The church has no name.
> Dead or dying plant—The church is dying.

Comment: The leadership needs to hear this.

In summary, leaders must take their positions seriously. The Lord is not pleased with those who commit themselves to becoming leaders and then misuse or misrepresent the ministry.

> And that servant who knew his master's will, and did not prepare himself or do according to his will, shall be beaten with many stripes. But he who did not know, yet committed things deserving of stripes, shall be beaten with few. For everyone to whom much is given, from him much will be required; and to whom much has been committed, of him they will ask the more (Luke 12:47–48).

> "Not everyone who says to Me, 'Lord, Lord,' shall enter the kingdom of heaven, but he who does the will of My Father in heaven. Many will say to Me in that day, 'Lord, Lord, have we not prophesied in Your name, cast out demons in Your name, and done many wonders in Your name?' And then I will declare to them, 'I never knew you; depart from Me, you who practice lawlessness!'" (Matt. 7:21–23).

CHAPTER 12

Warnings to the Nation

A common topic for prayer sessions is concern for the United States, especially on New Year's Eve or when calamity strikes somewhere in the nation. A number of my dreams and visions relate to the condition of the nation. The following is a short list of these dreams and visions.

Vision of the Trees
When: April 25, 1988
Where: Home during evening prayer for the nation.
Description: I saw an ear on a cup, followed by trees with ugly faces in their trunks. Then I saw a cup. The cup brought to mind a cup of fornication. Then I saw an elephant from the front. This was followed by an elephant sitting on a caldron. Then I saw an open dog's mouth as if howling and two upper teeth of an animal. Then I saw the dark black face of an idol. Finally, I saw a black gorilla face.

Interpretation:

>Ear on a cup—Listen to what the Spirit has to say.
>Trees with ugly faces—Humanity is offensive to My sight.
>Cup—They have drunk from the cup of fornication.
>Elephant—a great, powerful nation
>Elephant sitting on a caldron—The nation will suffer calamity.
>Open dog's mouth—There will be howling.
>Teeth—There will be gnashing of teeth.
>Dark black face of an idol—image of the beast
>Black gorilla face—the beast

Summary: Listen to what the Spirit has to say. Humanity has become offensive to My sight. They have drunk from the cup of fornication. The beast will cause calamity upon the earth. There will be howling and gnashing of teeth. Beware of the beast, and do not worship his image.

Comments: The interpretation seems to point more to the whole earth rather than just to the nation. The interpretation received a little help from two Bible passages:

And the word of the Lord came to me the second time, saying, "What do you see?" And I said, "I see a boiling pot, and it is facing away from the north." Then the Lord said to me: "out of the north calamity shall break forth on all the inhabitants of the land (Jer. 1:13–14).

He was granted power to give breath to the image of the beast, that the image of the beast should both speak and cause as many as would not worship the image of the beast to be killed (Rev. 13:15).

Vision of Snow
When: September 8, 1988
Where: Home
Background: I received this vision in the morning after awakening from a dream about ice.
Description: There were three scenes shown to me. They were of a cold, freezing winter. They went in sequence, as if a camera was moving from point to point from the same location, pausing momentarily at each scene. I got the impression that the first scene was to the north, the second scene was to the east, and the third scene was to the south. The first scene was that of a steep hill or mountain covered with ice and snow. It gave the feeling of extreme cold. The next scene was the edge of a forest with lots of snow in the foreground. The last scene (although tough to recall) seemed to be a large, open field of snow.
Interpretation:

> Mountain, snow, and cold—The government will encounter a serious economic crisis.

Trees and snow—Industry will come to a standstill.

Field and snow—Food will be scarce.

Summary: The vision seems to indicate poverty and famine are on the horizon.

Vision of the Tripod
When: Morning, December 21, 1988
Where: MBCF
Description: I saw a white, large, shallow bowl on a golden tripod. The bowl appeared to have water in it and looked like the top of the birdbath I have at home. Then I saw a colorful Christmas tree ornament, followed by a colorful Oriental lamp. Then I saw an Arabian head covering. I saw hands with eight fingers showing and then two thumbs together. Then I saw dark clouds with a cloud of rocket exhaust in the foreground. This was followed by a carved wooden eagle standing upright (in totem pole fashion). Then I saw an eagle falling forward, followed by a spinning bicycle wheel. This was followed by a bicycle wheel trying to be raised or lowered.
Interpretation:

> Golden tripod with a bowl—a divine (gold) look into the future
> Christmas ornament—Christmas time
> Oriental lamp—East
> Arabian head covering—Middle East
> Eight fingers—Destruction

Two thumbs together—Pressure
Dark clouds—a time of trouble
Rocket exhaust—economy going up in smoke
Eagle falling—The United States will fall.
Bicycle wheel spinning—Industrial or economic power
Bicycle wheel trying to be raised or lowered—struggling economy

Comment: This is a bit difficult to interpret. Generally eight is the number of salvation. However, in terms of the beast, it means the opposite: destruction. The Christmas ornament probably means a Christmas message. The vision occurred on the Sunday before Christmas.

Summary: During a future Christmas, there will be trouble from the Middle East. The United States' economy will fall. It will struggle to regain its position.

Vision of the Bottle
When: September 15, 2001, during Saturday morning prayer
Where: Faith Chapel
Background: Men were praying for the nation and the situation surrounding the planes hitting the twin towers and the Pentagon.
Description: I saw a clear bottle that was rectangular in shape with a small neck. The bottom of the bottle was not solid but moved like the motion of a hot water bottle. Then the

whole bottle became solid and was being filled with water from a tap. The next scene showed a hand with part of the arm showing. A cup was in the hand. I looked into the cup and couldn't see anything except for triangular pieces around the inside of the rim of the cup. The cup was lifted, as if someone was drinking from it. Then I saw a wine goblet.

Interpretation:

> Bottle—the nation
> Non-solid bottom—The nation is not standing firm in the Lord.
> Narrow neck—narrow minded, perhaps stiff-necked
> Completely solid bottle—The nation needs to stand firm in the Lord.
> Bottle being filled with water—The nation needs to be filled with the Spirit.
> Cup with triangular pieces—strength from the Father, Son, and Holy Spirit
> Wine goblet—Word of God

Summary: The nation is not standing firm on the Lord. They are a narrow-minded, stiffed-necked people. The nation needs to stand firm on the Lord and be filled with the Spirit. Drink of the cup of strength from the Father, Son, and Holy Spirit, for in it is the Word of God.

Vision on Mixing with the World
When: March 7, 2008
Where: Small group coaches meeting
Description: There appeared something like chocolate pudding that was just stirred. Then I saw a drop of a white substance that gave the impression that it was the last drop to go into the mix. Then a glass filled with water appeared. Then I saw a small, narrow, yellow, rectangular box standing on its end with triangular flags or pendants protruding from the top. The flags were being drawn back into the top of the box, as if the festivities were ending. Then I saw a partially built house made of sections of blocks (almost like Legos) with bright yellow, red, and blue colors. Then I saw a glass of water, followed by light pink and blue two-dimensional balloons that were rising. Then I saw what appeared to be chocolate pudding being stirred.
Interpretation:

> Stirred chocolate pudding and white substance—mixing with the world
> Last drop—end of mixing
> Glass with water—repent or perhaps be filled with the Spirit
> Box on end—Things have come to an end.
> Flags being withdrawn—The festivities are over.
> Partially built house—Build your house.
> Three colors—Trinity; Father, Son, and Holy Spirit

Glass of water—repent or perhaps be filled with the Spirit
Balloons—celebration
Pudding being stirred—mixing

Summary: The time has come to stop mixing with the world. Repent. Be filled with the Holy Spirit. The party has come to an end. It's time to build a house in the name of the Father, Son, and Holy Spirit. Repent. Be filled with the Holy Spirit and celebrate! Do not mix with the world.
Comment: I had trouble interpreting the box and the house. I finally asked the Lord three weeks later to reveal the interpretation. The Lord answered immediately.

Dream about Waves
When: October 3, 1989
Where: Home
Description: I was on a ship and was looking for sharks to shoot. The water was rough, and I told a lady on the ship that the water was too rough to shoot sharks. They were at too great of a distance. Then I saw huge plates of water rising at the starboard (right) side of the ship. One big wave turned into the shape of an elephant. We were then passing near a town. The same plate-like waves were seen next to the town. The next scene had me riding in a car with a friend who was an acoustician. I saw a tornado in front of us on the road. My friend steered off the road into a desert-like terrain at high speed and didn't slow

down. Although the desert appeared rough, it was a smooth ride.

Interpretation:

>   Ship—church
>   Sea—world
>   Sharks—predators, antichrists
>   Lady on the ship—bride of Christ
>   Elephant—beast
>   Right side of ship—righteous
>   Town—dwelling place
>   Friend who was acoustician—sound
>   Tornado—destruction
>   Desert—wilderness, protection

Summary: The church is struggling in a world full of turmoil and finding it difficult to defend the bride of Christ against the threat of antichrists. The beast is at war against the righteous. The place in which you dwell is not safe. It is the road to destruction. The sound solution is to take you into the wilderness, where I can protect you.

Comments: This interpretation seems to coincide with a passage in the book of Revelation.

Therefore rejoice, O heavens, and you who dwell in them! Woe to the inhabitants of the earth and the sea! For the devil has come down to you, having great wrath, because he knows that he has a short time." Now when the dragon saw that he had been cast to the earth, he persecuted the woman who gave birth to the male Child.

But the woman was given two wings of a great eagle, that she might fly into the wilderness to her place, where she is nourished for a time and times and half a time, from the presence of the serpent ... And the dragon was enraged with the woman, and he went to make war with the rest of her offspring, who keep the commandments of God and have the testimony of Jesus Christ (Rev. 12:12–14, 17).

Dream about Upheavals
When: July 22, 1993
Where: Grand Canyon
Description: I was visiting a high school friend. He appeared drugged and had long hair. My attempts to get his attention were fruitless. I looked toward the ocean (Atlantic). The ocean was violent. I saw shapes of buttes/mesas being formed by the waves. They were rising and falling. Then I looked toward the shore. The shore was dark, as if it were night. I saw three or maybe four campfires.
Interpretation: A people I once knew have come under the influence of the world. They are intoxicated, and attempts to stir them to life have become futile. To get their attention, I will cause great upheavals in the nations, peoples, and tribes of the earth. The light shines in the darkness, but the darkness doesn't comprehend it.

Vision of Heavy Equipment
When: January 2011
Background: I was praying for a message to the people for 2011.
Description: I saw a yellow, heavy equipment vehicle with large tires. It was slowly moving along and maneuvering in muddy soil.
Interpretation: The wheels of industry will be slow and mired down because of the economy.

The general message to the nations, and especially to Christians, is to not mix with the world and to stay focused on the Lord. There appears to be a strong economic downturn on the horizon. It may occur before this book is published. This crisis could put the nation in the hands of the Antichrist.

The beast is rising from the sea. It's time for God's people to take Him seriously. They must fear God, come out of the world, and be filled with the Spirit. In the latter days, the Spirit will be poured out on our sons and daughters, according to the book of Joel. Who is ready to receive the Spirit? Who is willing to build his or her house for the Lord?

A lot of my dreams and visions seem to warn believers to be aware of the beast. The beast can be recognized through the character of Satan. Satan is a liar, murderer, deceiver, tormentor, hater of mankind, and lover of chaos. Jesus, on the other hand, demonstrates the characteristics of mercy, compassion, love, and joy, and He is our peace. People become like the god they worship. Those who worship Satan will be like him. Those who worship Jesus will be like Him.

The beast will appear as a wolf in sheep's clothing. He is the Antichrist. Those who kill Christians are antichrists and worship Satan. If a religion adopts Jesus as one of their prophets, then they must believe Him. Jesus said He was the way, the truth, and the life and that no man comes to the Father except through Him. If that's the case, then that religion must believe Him. And if they believe Him, then they must reject all beliefs that are counter to the holy Scriptures and the very character of Jesus.

CHAPTER 13

Spiritual Warfare and Deliverance

On many occasions when I am praying for individuals, the Lord will reveal a spiritual condition(s) by way of a vision. As mentioned early on, I received a vision during a prayer session in which one or more individuals had issues. The vision was of a mug of beer with a pair of scissors under it. It simply meant, "Cut out drinking beer." This was the solution to those in the session who had issues associated with a drinking problem.

The following vision was received when someone brought a lady into the men's prayer group who was basically picked up off a nearby street and was obviously in need of help in a spiritual sense. I received the following vision during prayer for the lady.

Vision Concerning Unclean Spirits
When: February 18, 2006, during Saturday morning prayer,
Where: Faith Chapel

Background: One of the members picked up a lady hitchhiker on his way to church and invited her to the prayer meeting.

Description: I saw a series of creatures: a dinosaur (T. Rex) with focus on its open mouth, a shark with focus on its mouth open, and an alligator of sorts with its mouth open. The focus was on the large, open mouths of these creatures.

Interpretation: These were devouring, powerful, unclean spirits

Comment: When shaking hands with the lady visitor, I detected the odor of alcohol. She appeared to be a troubled lady. She left before we prayed for one another. The prayer for her was to bind the unclean spirits for a season to allow her the opportunity to receive the Lord as her Savior. I thought about this afterward and felt that I should have been a little bit bolder and simply commanded in the name of Jesus that all unclean spirits in her depart.

Years ago I read a book on spiritual warfare. The author described how a priest in Europe used the expression, "Depart in the name of Jesus," to drive out spirits from spiritually possessed people. He did this with boldness and with no doubt in his mind that the demons would depart.

One of my sons appeared to have a serious spiritual condition. After exhausting a number of avenues to correct the issue, one evening, just after I went to bed, I again prayed about the issue. The Lord reminded me about the book on spiritual warfare. In a bold manner of authority, I silently commanded in the name of Jesus that all demons in the house depart and not return. I did this silently so as to not wake up my wife. Immediately, my wife woke up and in a startled voice said that she heard the screams of a thousand demons. The next morning I talked to my son, who was preparing to go to school, and noticed a huge change in his nature. We actually had a real conversation.

It is one thing to point the finger at others (point out a splinter in another's eye), and it is another thing to pull the log out of my own eye. I chose to seek physical, mental, and emotional healing during a time of trouble. The first thing I did was to look at my own spiritual condition. During this time, the Lord gave me the following dream that showed me an interesting look at my family tree.

Dream about Birds
When: September 1996
Where: Home
Description: The scene appeared to be in the backyard of my home when I lived in Mattawamkeag, Maine. There were two trees. One stood to the left of me toward the north. The other stood in front of me toward the east. There were big, dark birds on the order of vultures in both of the trees. The trees had lots of limbs. The sky was gray, and the atmosphere was kind of dreary. The colors were shades of gray. In the tree to the left were lots of small birds on the order of doves sitting on the lower branches. The large birds appeared to be stationary and facing away from me. The smaller birds were active and facing toward me. I don't recall any small birds in the east tree, but I have a feeling they were there as well.

> **Interpretation**: The two trees represent my parents' family trees. The birds are unclean spirits. The large, stationary birds that were inactive and facing away from me didn't seem to be influencing me. They were facing toward past generations. Perhaps I didn't inherit the influence of these creatures. However, there were a number of smaller unclean spirits I might have inherited and that were currently active in my life. These unclean spirits or undesirable natures needed to be sought out and dealt with. An interesting point is that the name Mattawamkeag means "river with many rocks at the mouth." Perhaps there are many rocks impeding the flow of the Spirit within me and perhaps not.

There were other times when I would sense an evil presence in the house, especially at night. This evil presence would strike great fear in me. When I demanded in the name of Jesus that the unclean spirit(s) depart from the house, a great peace would come over me and all fear would depart. I always followed up with a request that angels of the Lord Jesus would encamp around me and prevent the influence of unclean spirits from entering the house.

One day during men's prayer, an individual came in with obvious spiritual problems. He had what appeared to be Tourette syndrome. He would tense up and make odd throat sounds, and he had a tendency to curse. He spoke of going to psychics and witches, and he believed they put curses on him. They touched him with pentagrams and other objects. Following prayer, some felt that several demons departed from him, but the stronghold demon remained. Toward the end of the session, I saw the following vision.

Vision of the Ropes
When: April 8, 2000, during Saturday morning men's prayer meeting
Where: Faith Chapel
Description: I saw a long, gold band like that of an ancient Egyptian or Babylonian ruler/warrior on a man's right forearm. There was a dark design on the band that was outlined in gold. The next scene was of two coils of rope, one on the upper forearm and one on the lower forearm. They were bound together by the same rope.
Interpretation:

> Gold band—Egyptian/Babylonian
> Black design on gold band—occult
> Two ropes—two demonic strongholds
> Ropes tied together—the strongholds are tied together in some way

Comment: The man who came to the prayer meeting seemed to be under the spell of a spirit named David. Also, he mentioned that his girlfriend had recently broken up with him. The demonic spirit seemed to curse and rise up when he spoke of his girlfriend leaving him. He mentioned that he was diagnosed with Tourette syndrome.
Summary: It appeared that his hatred toward his girlfriend leaving him was tied to some other

stronghold, something he either experienced or inherited. It could be that in his visits to the psychics and witches, he picked up a strong demon associated with the ancient occult. Pentagrams are used by the occult to direct forces and energies, and they are associated with Satanism. In my opinion, our prayer group was not geared to be a deliverance ministry per se.

Vision on Astrology
When: May 16, 1988, during morning prayer
Where: MBCF
Background: I was praying against astrology in the manner of spiritual warfare.
Description: I saw a missile being launched with a nosecone in the shape of a wizard's hat. (The hat was black with a moon and stars on it.) The vision focused on the hair sticking out at the base of the hat. The hair was black, unkempt, short, and straight.
Interpretation:

> Wizard's hat—astrology
> Hair—witchcraft
> Missile—spiritual warfare

Summary: Spiritual warfare needs to be launched against astrology and witchcraft.

The Christian church appears to not put a whole lot of effort into dealing with the powers of darkness to the degree that they should. Prayer sessions should involve conducting spiritual warfare, not necessarily every time Christians meet, but it should be scheduled on occasion or many occasions. Deliverance ministries should be commonplace. The church shouldn't allow the defeated enemy to steal the victory that Christ won for them on the cross.

CHAPTER 14

Seeing into the Future

Following are a few dreams that showed events that occurred in the future and one dream that pointed to a disaster in the making.

Dream Foretelling a New Project

As mentioned earlier, while serving as a test director on a ship, I dreamed about mobilizing another ship for another project. Prior to that time, I had made up my mind that I would not get involved in another sea test. When I returned home, my supervisor asked me to take over another project and get involved in the mobilization of a new ship. With some arm twisting, I reluctantly agreed. While on site, my photographer wanted a better view of the operations. I led him to the second story of a vacant warehouse. To my surprise, the view of the operations was exactly what was in my dream. I suspected that the Lord had something in mind for having me involved in the project. This may have something to do with the next dream.

Dream Foretelling Entering a Foreign Port

While participating in a project at sea, I dreamed of being at a port city and having to surrender my passport in order to visit the city. A lady in our group handled the passports and was given a difficult time by the port authorities. Arriving at that port city was not in our original plan. However, a storm and the need for ship repairs forced us to visit the nearest port. While waiting for repairs, we decided to go ashore and visit the city. The city was the one in my dream. A lady in our group (the same lady as in the dream) worked with the port authorities, and as in the dream, she handled getting our group's passports and was having a difficult time dealing with the authorities.

While in the city, I visited an old church that contained an old mosaic depicting Christ and two apostles. I could see compassion and other emotions in the way the figures were depicted in the mosaic. I have often wondered if this was the reason for the dream and entering this particular port. Another reason could be that as the ship passed Islamic towns and cities, the Lord wanted me to pray that the light of Jesus would shine on them. This is a common practice for me when taking ocean voyages on cruise ships.

Dream about Two Bears
When: Late March 2000
Where: Home
Description: I was tracking someone who ran into the woods, and I was on a hill. Then I heard snoring. I saw a bear in front of me digging his way out of the ground. Then I heard snoring to my right. It appeared to be a bear waking up.

Interpretation: The stock market will become a bear market. Given two bears (two witnesses), the stock market will crash.

Comment: My research shows that a bear market occurred that same month and continued through October 2002. Some analysts claim it ended in March 2003.

Dream about a Tidal Wave
When: July 2007
Where: Home
Description: I was on the seashore and saw a huge wave (ten stories or higher) coming in from the ocean. As I turned to run inland, I saw a similar huge wave coming from the land. I could see that there was no escape. I was caught in the middle. I ran toward a building and began running down the hallway in the building toward the wave coming in from the land. I stopped and climbed as high as I could on bookshelf-like steps. As I turned and looked down, there were men with beards and partially bald heads equally spaced and walking in the direction toward the inland wave. The men looked exactly the same as they passed me. They looked at me in a puzzling yet intimidating stare, as if they were wondering why I was not going with them.

Interpretation: The wave in the ocean was the beast that rose from the sea or perhaps a major economic crisis. The wave on the land was the beast that rose from the land. The people who were walking toward the land were Christians of like mind, seeking safety with the beast that rose from the land. They are those who were deceived by the Antichrist and will take the mark of the beast. They were puzzled as to why I did not join them.

Comment: This dream seems to have a parallel (or double) meaning. First, it is a warning to not be deceived by the Antichrist. Don't flee from one beast to go toward the other. Don't let the world use one crisis to lead you to another. Second, about three months later, another bear market occurred (October 2007). It ended around March 2009.

A few days before the market began its fall, I dreamed of a tidal wave (I didn't record the dream). A news commentator described the situation as a financial tsunami. I never heard that term before and couldn't help but recall the dream I had a few days earlier. The dream was a warning.

However, the dream about two tidal waves indicates that the financial crisis will drive people to a major change that will offer hope after a major calamity. That major calamity is yet to come. At this point (as of December, 2010), we are experiencing what is called a bear rally. Some analysts will call it a bull market. I believe this bear rally will be overtaken by a significant drop in the stock market matching a trend that occurred in the 1929 crash.

When the drop occurs, the country may not be able to recover as it did before. This will give the Antichrist an opportunity to step in, take advantage of the crisis, and gain control on a global scale, as the crisis will be worldwide.

As pointed out in visions concerning the United States, the country is warned to beware of the beast.

Dream of September 4
When: January 22, 2011
Where: Carnival cruise ship
Description: I was working on a classified project in a North Korean plant. At the end of my shift, I left the plant. As I left, I noticed that my clothes were gone, and I was walking in my underwear. The indication was that whatever I was working on contaminated my clothes, and I was directed to another area to get a new set of clothes. People around me didn't think it unusual to get a new set of clothes. The date September 4 was mentioned. Then the expression "not September 5, but September 4" was emphasized. No year was given.

Comment: It's one thing to look back and see if a vision or dream line up with a subsequent event, and it's another thing to predict into the future that something is going to occur on a specific date. On one hand, if it occurs, I can say, "See, I told you so." On the other hand, if I'm wrong, I'll be stoned as a false prophet. However, given that the year was not specified, I'm somewhat protected from getting stoned. In either case, the dream appears to be a warning.

Dream about Selling Maps
When: Not sure
Background: I was planning to travel the next day on one of our map routes. (We had a side business that involved selling road maps.)

Description: In the dream, we were selling maps to one of our customers.

Comment: The dream was a warning to not sell maps to this customer. The customer's business was shut down by the county, and the bill owed us was not paid. The issue with this dream was whether to take it as a warning or to build up our account with this customer. Discerning one way or the other was difficult.

Dream about an Oil Rig Disaster
When: February 14, 1982

Description: I was in a room on a platform of some sort at sea. Chaos and panic was breaking out as the platform was listing and about to fall into the sea. I remember focusing on one individual who was panic stricken and was yelling or perhaps screaming.

Comment: That morning I heard the news about the Newfoundland Oil Rig disaster in which the oil platform sank at sea with the loss of many lives. I was almost certain at the time that my dream related to that disaster and wondered if my dream occurred at the time the disaster was taking place. Many thoughts went through me that day, as I wondered if there was some spiritual connection with someone on board the platform that allowed me to witness the event. Knowing what I know now, the dream probably should have called for an immediate prayer of protection for the people on board the platform. In either case, I'm left with a still-frame image of the listing room with the panic-stricken individual.

These are just a few dreams that have come to pass as a help or direction to me or as a warning as to what is to take place.

CHAPTER 15

Prophecies Involving Personal Events

The following is a dream, a few visions, and a couple of thoughts that cover personal events.

Vision of a Seal
When: December 26, 1989
Where: Home
Background: We were worshipping the Lord with some friends from church.
Description: I saw an old car with the wheels filled in. Then I saw a tricycle with the large front wheel filled in. The filled-in region of the wheels was light yellow-orange in color. Then I saw a car headlight followed by a hand with five fingers holding a small, round seal that approached my forehead. Immediately, the Holy Spirit came upon me in a powerful way. As I thought about the seal placed upon God's anointed, the Holy Spirit

stayed with me. All this occurred during singing and worshipping the Lord.

Interpretation:

> Car with filled-in wheels—two wheels could be number of witness
> Tricycle—Trinity
> Big wheel—the Father
> Light yellow-orange color—I'm not sure, but it could be a color representing God similar to that described in Ezekiel.

As I sat in my house with the elders of Judah sitting before me, that the *hand of the Lord God fell upon me* there. Then I looked, and there was a likeness, like the *appearance of fire*—from the appearance of His waist and downward, fire; and from His waist and upward, like the *appearance of brightness, like the color of amber* (Ezek. 8:2).

> Headlight—Logic and reasoning
> Hand with five fingers—hand of ministry
> Seal—seal of God with the Father's name on it (see verses below)

They were commanded not to harm the grass of the earth, or any green thing, or any tree, but only those men who do not have the seal of God on their foreheads (Rev. 9:4).

Then I looked, and behold, a Lamb standing on Mount Zion, and with Him one hundred and forty-four thousand, having His Father's name written on their foreheads (Rev. 14:1).

Summary: I pondered on this vision for quite some time. I wondered if it meant that I have the seal of approval to minister for the Lord because of my logic and reasoning associated with the holy Scriptures. I would certainly accept the idea of being sealed with the Father's name on my forehead. I'm not sure what the filled-in wheels mean. It could mean the inner circle of completeness. Perhaps the two wheels represent the inner circle of completeness of the Son and the Holy Spirit and that the three bear witness of the sealing. There's lots of speculation here.

> For there are three that bear witness in heaven: the Father, the Word, and the Holy Spirit; and these three are one (1 John 5:7).

Whatever it means, at the time of the vision, it appears that I had the Lord's favor.

The Two Swords
In the early nineties, I inquired as to the meaning of the two swords mentioned in Luke 22:38. The Lord responded with two words: *logos* and *rhema*. Logos means "a thing uttered or expressed in words[1]." Rhema means "that which is spoken[2]." Basically, the two swords represent the voice of God. This may explain the two-edged sword coming out of the mouth of the figure described in Revelation 1. Words come out of the mouth.

During the end times, the last two witnesses will minister with the voice of God, the two swords: *logos* and *rhema*. As mentioned in Ephesians 6, the spiritual sword (*rhema*) is used against the rulers of the darkness of this age and against spiritual hosts of wickedness in the heavenly places.

The Antichrist will counterfeit this with two swords of his own. It is interesting to note that two swords were found in Iraq associated with Saddam Hussein. This is the site of ancient Babylon. The symbol of the Muslim Brotherhood is the book of Allah (the Quran) between two swords. The swords symbolize jihad and the force that protects the words in "Allah's book." As mentioned in the Quran (Sura 8:12), they are physical swords that are used to sever heads and cut off fingers.

Dream about Investing in African Oil
When: February 7, 2011

Background: I was contemplating purchasing stock in an oil company that had interest in a block off the coast of West African. A financial analyst was saying that the long-term return on investment was thirty-five times the current value.

Description: I was serving as a waiter in what appeared to be an upscale restaurant. A well-dressed, well-to-do black man who had tipped me quite well handed me some extra cash as he got up from the table. He looked on as I handed my assistant $35.

Interpretation: The black man stood for a wealthy area of Africa (perhaps the oil block). The extra tip was a stock tip. The $35 associated the tip with the stock that I was contemplating buying.

Comment: I questioned whether this dream was a warning to not buy the stock, or perhaps it was a nod to go ahead and purchase the stock. The clue that made me decide to purchase the stock was the handing of the $35 to my assistant. I was managing my brother's stock account. This sort of meant that two people would benefit from the purchase if I was to purchase stock for him. Within a week, we both capitalized on the investment. However, it was not a thirty-five-fold return on our investment. The company was bought out a very short time later. It's good to have the Lord by your side. It's also good to tithe. It has its benefits.

Vision of the Electronic Timing
Where: Home, during evening prayer
Background: My car engine was intermittently quitting while driving. I couldn't figure out what the problem was, so I simply asked the Lord for a solution.
Description: I saw a clock in the shape of a cuckoo clock, followed by electric arcing similar to small lightning bolts over the clock.
Interpretation: I wasn't sure what this meant until my mechanic said that he suspected the problem was a chip that electronically controlled the timing. I didn't know that the car had such a device, as this was new technology being introduced at the time. He said the part was $90 to replace but he couldn't guarantee that it would solve the problem. I told him to go ahead with the fix, as in my mind I knew that it would solve the

problem based on the vision I had. Incidentally, it did solve the problem.

Comment: This is an example of asking the Lord to help solve a problem and the Lord responding with a solution.

And whatever things you ask in prayer, believing, you will receive (Matt. 21:22).

Vision of the Bolt and Washer

Where: At home, in the evening by myself by the pool

When: July 1996

Background: I was seeking an uplifting word from the Lord, as I was feeling a bit down and felt abandoned. I needed a shot in the arm.

Description: I saw a bolt and washer. The threads looked like they had been painted white, but the paint was worn, as if the bolt had been used. The washer was thick and slanted at the center of the bolt. The bolt had a hex head, and the hex head changed to a round head with no grooves for a screwdriver.

Interpretation: I puzzled over this vision that evening. The next morning, I was just leaving home in my van when I noticed that the right side mirror was loose. I had just tightened it the day before. I had trouble tightening it and wondered why the bolt would not tighten down enough to secure the mirror in place. As I drove along, I remembered that the bolt threads looked liked the bolt threads in the vision. I later looked at the bolt and found that the bolt had broken off in the insert and would not tighten beyond the broken piece. The solution to fix the problem was to put a thick washer on the bolt. The bolt had a spline-type head that was difficult to turn because I didn't have the right tool. The solution was to replace the bolt with one that was shorter and had a hex head. However, it didn't matter, as the washer did the trick, and if it loosened again, I would purchase a hex head bolt.

Comment: I believe that the Lord was telling me several things besides telling me how to fix the problem. First, the Lord knows my needs. Second, He is listening to my prayers. And third, the Lord has not abandoned me. This is an example of the Lord knowing our needs before we ask Him.

For your Father knows the things you have need of before you ask Him (Matt. 6:8).

Thought and Vision While Selling a House
When: August 2008
Background: We were selling our house in California and moving to Tucson at the time of the housing crisis. (House prices were in a steep downtrend.) There was an offer on the house that was a bit too low, and we were trying to decide what to counteroffer.
Description: As I was standing in the living room, the Lord placed on my mind to go running. I believe it was a Sunday. My five-mile run on the weekend included a road that passed a golf course.

Along the way, I would find golf balls. I didn't golf, but a couple of my friends at work did, and I would collect the golf balls for them. I usually would find two or three balls along the route. A half a dozen was an excellent find.

Before running, the Lord placed upon my mind to set the counteroffer based on the number of golf balls I found during the run. I don't recall exactly what value I placed on each ball, but one of the higher values was placed on finding ten golf balls and a much lower number was placed on finding eleven or more balls.

Comment: I was amazed to find ten golf balls as I passed the golf course. As I set the counteroffer in my mind, my thought was that it may be a bit high, but I decided to trust in the Lord on this. Lo and behold, as I continued running, another golf ball appeared in a place that one would not expect to find one.

We set the price, which, by the way, was quite reasonable, based on the golf ball find. The buyer countered within $5,000 of our counteroffer. My wife wanted to accept the counteroffer, but I insisted on waiting on the Lord before making a decision. While laying down, I received a vision that indicated we should split the offer. The buyer agreed to the split, and as a result, we profited an extra $2,500 on the transaction. There were many other such incidences during the house sale that indicated the Lord was supporting us in a big way on selling our house. For example, the buyer saw the house the day the for-sale sign went up, before it went into the multiple listing service. Incidentally, after the sale, the value of the house dropped about $100,000 as the housing market continued on its downward trend.

Dream about a Rock Spider
When: Late 1980s
Where: Home
Description: I didn't record this dream, but I remember dreaming about a rock spider on a Sunday morning. Upon awakening, I thought about the dream and wondered if a rock spider actually existed and what it looked like. In my search, it turned out that a rock spider was an Australian term for a petty thief that robs amorous couples in parks or by the sea shore. It is also Australian prison slang for a pedophile (child molester). I didn't know about its use as prison slang at the time.

Prior to the morning church service, I noticed an individual entering the church. He seemed a bit strange. I made a point to introduce myself and welcome him to the church. We struck up a conversation, and it wasn't too long before I was able to figure out that he was a drifter. From the conversation, it was obvious that this person couldn't be trusted. Then the words "rock spider" came to mind. It was like a warning. I pointed him out to one of the elders and warned the ushers of his presence. They kept a close eye on him, and I never saw him again.

Comment: Although my actions could be perceived as a bit judgmental, I felt at the time that as a watchman, the Lord provided me with the gift of discernment. I ran the sound booth at the back of the sanctuary for several years. I always considered watching over the congregation as part of my job. Incidentally, one of the questions the individual asked pertained to the location of the young children's Sunday school classes. At the time, I thought that it was a strange question to be asked. Perhaps the prison slang for rock spider (child molester) was more appropriate.

Helping Me Find Fabric
When: July 2010
Where: Fabric store, Seattle, Washington
Description: My wife and I were searching for fabric in preparation for a wedding. We had pretty much exhausted our search for the particular fabric we were looking for. I saw some shelves in the back corner of the store, checked one side of the shelf, and determined that it was a waste of time to search anymore. As I stood in the aisle by the shelf, the Lord placed on my mind a story that Pastor Pamela told about finding a purple carpet for the church. Unknown to the owner of the carpet store, there was a purple roll of carpet in the back corner of the store. Pastor Pamela had a premonition to check the back corner of the store. There she found the carpet. I had my doubts about finding the fabric, but I decided to play this out. I checked the other side of the shelf, and lo and behold, there was the exact fabric my wife was looking for.

Dream about a Rattlesnake
When: March 7, 2011
Where: Home, Tucson
Background: I had written an article comparing the two swords used in the symbol of the Muslim Brotherhood to the two swords mentioned in Luke

22:38 and was going to offer it to the *Christian Post* for publication.

Description: I was tapping on a short pile of papers with a small stick. There was a rattlesnake under the papers. It appeared to be quite irritated with me. I could clearly see his head. He was a mean-looking rattlesnake. He was looking at me, more like glaring at me. He came out from under the pile of papers and began to move toward me. He landed on the cement of a driveway in front of a garage. It was a sunny day. As I quickly backed up, he began to quickly move toward me.

Interpretation:

> Papers—Christian writings
> Snake—the enemy
> Tapping of the papers—My writings are irritating the enemy.
> Snake attacking me—the enemy attacking me
> Driveway—drive him away

Comment: I recently wrote an article for the *Christian Post* that was published. I published my book *Genesis 1* about eight months ago and have finished the first draft of this book. This second article that was going to be offered to the *Christian Post* appears to have stimulated the dream. The dream appears to be a warning. My article must have irritated Satan. The simple solution was to pray and ask the Lord for protection. I believe He will protect me. I must be bold like a lion and serve the Lord to the best of my ability. I must not fear the enemy. As it says in Proverbs, the fear of the Lord is the beginning of wisdom. By the way, the *Christian Post* published the second article.

These are just a few of the dreams and visions that have come to pass as a help, direction, or a warning.

(1) Harold K. Moulton, *The Analytical Greek Lexicon Revised*, The Zondervan Corporation, Grand Rapids, Michigan, 1978, Page 249.
(2) Ibid, Page 359.

CHAPTER 16

End-Time Prophecies

The following visions and dreams point to end-time events such as famine, locusts, the beast, and turmoil.

> **Vision of the Crystal**
> **When:** September 21, 1988, morning
> **Where**: Home
> **Background**: Some friends of mine prophesied that a famine was approaching. I asked the Lord for the timing on the famine.
> **Description**: I saw a crystal, and then I saw a clock set at 12:00.
> **Interpretation**: I'm not sure—perhaps the year 2012.
>
> **Vision of the Dragon**
> **When:** September 29, 2001, Saturday morning prayer
> **Where**: Faith Chapel

Description: I saw a stormy sea with land and houses in the background. A portion of the sea began to rise and take the shape of the back of a gigantic whale. The head was not visible. Along the backbone was a series of small plates or scales like that of a dragon. I looked for the head and tail and thought I saw the tail of a whale. In the next scene, I saw a large, bright red house with a sloping roof. The focus seemed to be on the roof. The next scene was that of a Quonset hut.
Interpretation:

> Stormy sea—nations, peoples in turmoil
> Sea monster—the beast is rising up out of the sea.
> Scales like that of a dragon—associated with dragon
> Red—blood or danger
> Roof—covering
> Quonset hut—shelter

Summary: During this time of turmoil in the nations, a beast associated with the dragon (Satan) is rising up. Do not fear, for My blood is your covering and shelter during this storm.
Comment: The first beast of Revelation 13 rises from the sea. This vision occurred just over two weeks after 9/11.

A year later, I had a dream about a dragon.

Vision of the Eye of the dragon

When: September 22, 2002, evening service

Where: Faith Chapel

Background: I had been reading Jeremiah 13 and 14 that day and transcribing some tapes on Revelation for Pastor Graham Truscott during the week.

Description: I saw what appeared to be the eye of a dragon. It was open. Then I saw an image of a king imbedded in a rock. The rock was gray in color. The king had a crown with three points on it. My thought was that it was King Midas. Then I saw faint sketches of a fishhook. Eventually, a clear fishhook appeared. It began to move around very quickly or perhaps whipped about very quickly. This image transitioned into what appeared to be a fine wire entanglement and eventually, a spiraling wire with a sharpened gray-colored lead pencil with the typical metal and eraser on top in the midst of it. The next image was a swordfish that was beautiful in color. As I thought of the image as perhaps being interpreted as a sword, the image reappeared again with a more intense look at the swordfish.

Interpretation:

>Dragon—Satan

So the great dragon was cast out, that serpent of old, called the Devil and Satan, who deceives the whole world; he was cast to the earth, and his angels were cast out with him (Rev. 12:9).

> King embedded in a rock—image of the beast

And he [second beast, false prophet] deceives those who dwell on the earth by those signs which he was granted to do in the sight of the beast, telling those who dwell on the earth to make an image to the beast who was wounded by the sword and lived (Rev. 13:14).

> Crown with three points—three unclean spirits; dragon, beast, and false prophet

And I saw three unclean spirits like frogs coming out of the mouth of the dragon, out of the mouth of the beast, and out of the mouth of the false prophet (Rev. 16:13).

> King Midas—power to do miracles, such as turning things into gold

He [second beast, false prophet] performs great signs, so that he even makes fire come down from heaven on the earth in the sight of men. And he deceives those who dwell on the earth by those signs which he was granted to do in the sight of the beast ... (Rev. 13:13–14).

> Fishhook, moving, wire entanglement–snaring
> No. 2 pencil with spiraling wire around it–ensnaring witnesses

And the dragon was enraged with the woman, and he went to make war with the rest of her offspring, who keep the commandments of God and have the testimony of Jesus Christ (Rev. 12:17).

> Beautiful swordfish—bride of Christ, Christians
>
> Sword—Word of God

And take the helmet of salvation, and the sword of the Spirit, which is the word of God (Eph. 6:17).

Summary: The open eye means that the dragon (Satan) is awake. His false prophet has made an image of the beast that rose from the sea. Three unclean spirits will come out of his mouth. He will have the power to perform miracles to deceive the very elect. He will attempt to hook and ensnare Christians who have the Word of God on their forehead.

Vision of the Musical Instrument
When: January 19, 2003, during the second service
Where: Faith Chapel
Description: I saw ghostlike hands playing a musical instrument. The musical instrument was not in detail enough to determine its type, but from the placement of the hands, it could be a clarinet. There was a break or interruption in the

service, and the vision continued later on during worship. I saw ghostlike hands on each side of a gift-wrapped package. The first two scenes were in grayscale colors. The next scene was a cylindrical-shaped bomb with a short fuse that was lit. The bomb was angled toward me with an emphasis on the short fuse that was burning.

Interpretation:

> Ghostlike hands—Holy Spirit
> Musical instrument—announcing something
> Bomb—explosion
> Short fuse—explosion to happen shortly

Summary: In a short time, the Holy Spirit will hand out a gift that will cause an explosion within the church and will in turn cause church growth.

Vision of the Gifts
When: January 4, 2008
Where: Small groups coaches meetings
Description: I saw a large roll of brown wrapping paper on a spool like the ones found in a store for wrapping stuff. Then I saw a gift wrapped in the same color wrapping paper with a ribbon of earthly tones blending well with the color of the wrapping paper. The ribbon went across and up and down the package. The center of the roll of wrapping paper seemed to be spinning fast. The roller and paper toward the center moved

in and out of the roll as if the roll was spinning fast. It sort of reminded me of a spinning lathe. I saw this movement twice, as if the Lord was placing emphasis on the fact that the paper roll was spinning fast. A white face mask with red stripes appeared. The stripes looked like they were brushed on in a random fashion. Then I saw a large metallic silver/gray pitcher pouring something. A steam locomotive appeared. Donald Duck appeared up close with focus on his bill. Then Daffy Duck appeared at a distance with a black background with focus on his orange bill. A black dial-type telephone appeared. Then I saw the face of a man with hands in front of the face as if in prayer.

Interpretation:

> Fast-spinning roll of paper and gift—Many gifts are being quickly wrapped.
> Mask—The gifts are to be secretly distributed.
> Red stripes—Perhaps by My stripes you were healed. Maybe the gifts are of a healing nature.
> Pitcher—The gifts are to be poured out on the brethren.
> Steam locomotive—to demonstrate the power of the Holy Spirit
> Cartoon characters with focus on bills—I don't have a clue what this is.
> Telephone—Call upon the Lord.
> Man praying—Pray for the gifts.

Summary: Gifts of the Holy Spirit are quickly being prepared and will secretly be poured out, demonstrating the power of the Holy Spirit. We must call upon the Lord and ask Him for these gifts.

Dream about the Rust-Colored Horse
When: March 16, 1989
Description: I was looking toward the garden, and I saw a beautiful rust-colored horse. The horse was small but very muscular. It moved with great speed and ran in front of me and around to the back side of some tall, narrow plants. It immediately chomped off the tops of the tall plants and ran in front of me and away. I turned to look where he went, and I saw a beautiful white horse and a beautiful rust-colored horse lying side by side in a field to the south of the garden. There were people milling around to the right of me. I was on the west side of the garden. They didn't seem to know what was going on.
Comment: This dream reminds me of the red horse in the book of Revelation that sets out to take peace from the earth.

Another horse, fiery red, went out. And it was granted to the one who sat on it to take peace from the earth, and that people should kill one another; and there was given to him a great sword (Rev. 6:4).

The tall plants could be national leaders who are about to be removed. It will happen quickly. The white horse in Revelation set out to conquer. Its task was finished, and it was resting. I wonder if the current removal of leaders from Islamic nations like Egypt, Libya, and Tunisia are steps toward removing peace from the earth. Organizing the Islamic nations under the Muslim Brotherhood (a caliphate, as some would call it) could set the stage to remove peace and create chaos. The Muslim religion has a strong anti-Semitism and anti-Christian flavor to it. There is a definite end-time connotation here.

Dream about the Four Horses
When: around July 6, 2008
Description: I was walking on a path and came to the edge of a high mountain. I saw a beautiful, expansive forest of green trees in the valley. I could see folds in the forest canopy, as if streams or gullies might be running through it. I could just barely make out the path through the large forest. As I continued to look, the valley appeared to be ancient, with indications of water erosion. I had hung on tight, as the path down the mountain was steep. While walking in the valley, I came to a wide, shallow stream. As I approached the stream, four horses with riders passed quickly in front of me on the shore closest to me. They went from right to left. It was a bright, shiny day. Upon reaching the bank of the stream, but still in the trees, I saw four more horses with riders

running quickly along the edge of the stream on the opposite side. They kicked up water as they ran. They also ran from right to left. I was being careful not to be spotted. As the last rider started around a bend in the stream, he spotted me and came back. In the next scene, the rider was trying to drown someone. The face of the victim appeared as a white, laughing, funny mask. The rider began to laugh and then appeared to have a heart attack.

Comment: This dream reminds me of the four seals that introduced the four horses in Revelation 6. Seeing two sets of four horses indicates that the seals may be broken and that the horses have been released or are about to be released. The fourth seal or horse is described in the following verse:

So I looked, and behold, a pale horse. And the name of him who sat on it was Death, and Hades followed with him. And power was given to them over a fourth of the earth, to kill with sword, with hunger, with death, and by the beasts of the earth (Rev. 6:8).

Perhaps the white mask stood for Christians who will laugh in the face of death and that death will have no power over them.

Vision of the Locust
When: July 5, 1988, during morning prayer
Where: MBCF
Description: I saw the following sequence of symbols: a locust, creepy creatures, the head of

a bug munching on something, various animals (from Africa), an old book, a bottle like that in *I Dream of Genie* (the bottle was moving about as if the contents were about to burst forth or be released, and the word "vial" came to mind), a martini glass with an eagle in background, the Lone Ranger riding his white horse, a hand, a hand with the palm up, a hand grasping something.

Interpretation:

> Locust, creepy creatures, bug—devouring
> African animals—location is Africa
> Old Book—Old Testament
> Bottle/vial—plague about to be poured out
> Martini glass/eagle—the nation is intoxicated
> Lone Ranger—High-ho silver away (wealth will be taken away)
> Hand with palm up—there will be begging for food
> Hand grasping something—hold on to what you have

Summary: A plague of locusts as seen in Egypt and described in the Old Testament is about to be poured out. The nation is intoxicated. Their wealth will be taken away, and the people will beg for food. Hold on to what you have.

Comment: The prayer leader mentioned the word "Joseph." This implies drought and famine. The question is when?

Dream about the Number Seven
When: September 20, 1988
Where: Home
Background: I was seeking an answer as to when the famine was going to occur. I had read the previous day about the famine in Egypt and Joseph's interpretation of Pharaoh's dreams.
Description: An earthquake occurred at home while I was away. A word from home said that it registered seven on the Richter scale.
Comment: This is difficult to understand, as a level-seven earthquake can cause severe damage. From a time point of view, there appeared to be no significant famine in 1995, seven years later. Why the number seven? Perhaps it means that the famine will begin when the San Diego area gets hit by a seven-point earthquake.

A couple of days later, I dreamed the following, which also involved the number seven.

Dream about Keys
When: September 22 or 23, 1988
Where: Home
Background: Prior to the dream, I was asking the Lord how many years it would be until the famine starts. Prior to this, I was receiving dreams and visions relating to events outlined in Revelation.
Description: My van was stuck in the sand. I was frustrated over getting help to free the van. In my frustration, I threw my keys down on the

ground. The keys scattered. As I picked them up, I counted them. The total was seven.

Comment: This is the second dream in which the number seven was emphasized. Incidentally, the number of keys on my key ring is seven. I wasn't aware of the number of keys on my key ring until now. Interesting! Perhaps there are seven keys to unlocking the answer. Seven is the number of divine completion. Perhaps something needs to be completed before the famine begins.

On November 27, 2010, as I finished reading these last two dreams in preparation for the book, I turned on the TV and switched to a Christian network. It was covering the story of Joseph and was at the point of interpreting the dreams of the butler and baker, followed by the interpretation of the Pharaoh's dream. Hmmm! Coincidence? This could be a clue as to when the drought/famine will begin.

The messages from the above visions and dreams indicate that the end-time prophecies are unfolding.

CHAPTER 17

NUTRITION

Sometimes the Lord seems to provide nutritional information when praying over individuals with different ailments or simply praying for nutritional advice. Many healings can take place from a simple change in diet. The following visions and dreams are samples of what I've experienced over the years.

Vision of the Apple
When: February 24, 1989
Where: MBCF
Background: The prayer topic was nutrition.
Description: I saw a perfectly shaped reddish apple with a stem in it. Bites were being taken out of the apple until only the core was left. Then I saw seeds of the core. Next I saw just the core of the apple.
Interpretation: Apples are good. Eat apples, a fruit that has seed in itself.

And the earth brought forth grass, the herb that yields seed according to its kind, and the tree that yields fruit, whose seed is in itself according to its kind. And God saw that it was good (Gen. 1:12).

Dream about Apples
When: I can't remember
Background: Seeking nutritional advice
Description: It seems like I was in the northwest part of the country, perhaps the state of Washington. I saw strawberries, and they were covered with debris and possibly bugs. Then I saw a lot of shiny, red apples. They were clustered very close together in the shape of a rectangular solid. They were really packed together.
Interpretation: The dream seems to discourage eating strawberries. (Their seed is not within itself.) It did encourage me to eat an abundance of apples and that they are packed with nutrition.
Comment: I didn't record this dream, but I remember it fairly well.

Dream about Honey
When: September 30, 1988
Description: I saw honey being processed. The honeycomb was being sliced, and it looked extremely appetizing.
Interpretation: I probably should add honey and perhaps honeycomb to my diet.

But while they still did not believe for joy, and marveled, He [Jesus] said to them, "Have you any

food here?" So they gave Him a piece of a broiled fish and some honeycomb. And He took it and ate in their presence
(Luke 24:41-43).

Dream about Eating Sweets
When: October 5, 1988
Description: I was tempted by sweets and took one of them. I was driving the van at the time. I noticed after eating the cookie or whatever it was, the van slowed down. I had lost concentration on what I was doing as I examined the tray of sweets.
Interpretation: I believe the Lord is telling me to stay away from processed sugars. They probably affect my alertness and concentration.

It is interesting to note that one dream indicated that honeycomb is good for you, but another dream discouraged me from eating sweets. I suspect that the ingredients in honeycomb (pollen, natural sugar) are good for you, but the processed sugar in sweets like candy are not very healthy for you. It's also interesting to note that the two dreams occurred within days of each other. Although not recorded, during the timeframe of the above dreams, I had a dream of white, processed sugar in a sugar bowl. The dream was basically telling me not to eat processed sugar.

About a month later, I was curious about why my system had trouble digesting pasta, and I received the following dream.

Dream about Spiders and the Yoke of an Egg
When: November 19, 1988

Description: It appears that I was conducting spiritual warfare. At the conclusion of this event, I entered a cave with small passages. The passages were blocked by spiders and spider webs. They were hungry, nasty-looking spiders. Then again, what spiders are not? I decided to leave. I threw a fly at one of the spiders, and it devoured it immediately. Someone who came with me left a cooked egg on a shelf in the cave. As I was leaving, the yolk of the egg was suspended in a web with a spider on it.

Comment: I was concerned the previous night about why I couldn't digest pasta (pasta being made of eggs and flour). The dream might have been telling me that egg yolks are not agreeable to my system and are detestable, like the flies that spiders eat. Hmm! Eliminating egg yolks could also reduce my cholesterol level.

Vision Concerning Prostrate Cancer
When: April 22, 2000, during Saturday morning men's prayer meeting
Where: Faith Chapel
Background: We were praying for two individuals who had high PSA counts and who were concerned about prostate cancer.
Description: I saw a hand holding a bundle or sheaves of grain. The word grain came to me.
Interpretation: Perhaps the Lord was saying that whole grains are needed to keep the PSA count low and offset the occurrence of prostate cancer.

As an interesting side note, I was visiting a friend with serious health issues the doctor(s) had a difficult time correcting. That afternoon, I was at the local library. Outside the library, I spotted a rack of books for sale. I decided to peruse through the books and came across a book titled *The Maker's Diet*. I purchased the book for ten cents. As I read the book, I discovered that the health issues that drove the author to write the book were very similar to the issues my friend was dealing with. I gave the book to my friend. To date, he hasn't read the book. It will be interesting to see if he reads the book, applies the recommended dietary changes, and regains his health.

The above dreams and visions indicate that the Lord is interested in our health. If we ask a question on health, the Lord is good to respond with an answer. It's one thing to receive an answer, and it's another thing to apply the answer to our lifestyle.

CHAPTER 18

CONCLUSION

The general theme of visions directed to individuals seems to be centered on peace. Jesus is the Prince of Peace. The Lord wants us to be filled with the Spirit and be at peace. We are to lift one another up and bring comfort and peace to each other. For example, if drinking beer causes turmoil, then cutting out beer is a step to replace turmoil with peace.

Visions directed to the congregation encourage people to be as wise virgins. The Lord wants us to continually work on cleaning out our vessels through the Word of God and to develop within ourselves the mind of Christ. An overriding theme is that He wants us to remove distractions in our lives, to be filled with the Spirit, and to communicate with Him on a regular basis.

Communication with the Lord is important because it gives the Lord the opportunity to demonstrate His love by helping you get through troubled times. Prayer is important. Also, we can clearly see that taking time to listen is equally important.

As for church leaders, it's fairly evident from the visions that the Lord is most unhappy with leaders who misrepresent Him to the congregation as well as the world. The Lord wants leaders to minister the Word to the unsaved in a spirit of humbleness and compassion. The messages to church leaders seem to be a reflection of what the Lord said concerning the seven churches described in the book of the Revelation of Jesus Christ.

Warnings to the nation and references to end-time events indicate that the prophecies that are foretold in the book of Revelation are unfolding. References to the dragon, the beast, drought, famine, and economic hard times are signs that point to the end of the age.

> He answered and said to them, "When it is evening you say, 'It will be fair weather, for the sky is red'; and in the morning, 'It will be foul weather today, for the sky is red and threatening.' Hypocrites! You know how to discern the face of the sky, but you cannot discern the signs of the times. A wicked and adulterous generation seeks after a sign, and no sign shall be given to it except the sign of the prophet Jonah" (Matt. 16:2–4).

The common nautical expression for this is, "Red sky at night, sailor's delight. Red sky in the morning, sailor's warning." The signs of the times Jesus was talking about pointed to His death and resurrection. Today the signs are pointing to the end times. The sky in the morning is red. The warning signs are here.

But what did the gift of visions do for me? Aside from the benefits of walking and talking with God, the gift of receiving visions has taken me to a whole new level of Christianity. When I was a child, I believed in God because my parents were Christians. I was born into Christianity and raised in the church. Over time, because of the lack of knowledge and understanding and worldly distractions, my faith in God diminished, and my belief in Him followed suit. It wasn't until my late twenties that I began to question life's existence. In the process of trying to find myself in the overall scheme of things, I began to research the existence of God. One thing led to another, and soon the evidence demanded a verdict. It was not on the level that Lee Strobel expressed in his book, *The Case for Christ,* but it was enough to convince me of the existence of God and that Jesus Christ was His Son and my Savior.

With this new level of faith, I had a great thirst for knowing and understanding the Word of God. The Lord knew my struggle in the learning process. Through circumstances determined by fate, the Lord led me to Restoration Temple, a church/school in San Diego headed by Dr. Graham Truscott. The church eventually changed its name to Mission Bay Christian Fellowship. It was a well-accredited Christian school at that time where I obtained my master's degree in biblical studies.

The increased level of education added a great deal to my faith. However, the real breakthrough to a higher level of Christianity came when the Lord began to communicate with me through visions and dreams, not to mention the benefits I received because of the visions. At this level, no force could shake my faith and belief in God. Does God exist? Most assuredly! Is Jesus Christ the only true way to eternal life? Most assuredly!

To the unbeliever whose heart and mind is clouded by the surrounding darkness, I beg that you repent of your sins and accept Jesus Christ as your Savior. His death on the cross gave everyone the opportunity to receive the gift of eternal life. Take the gift. It's free! The Lord paid the price for it. Let His light shine brightly in your heart and mind. You have nothing to lose and everything to gain. Don't reject it until you have at least tasted of its pleasures.

To the young and mature in Christ alike, I caution you to walk carefully, for deception is reaching out from every dark place to grab hold of what little you have. Do not forsake gathering together in a local church. The church is like a ship riding on the sea of nations. The Word of God will serve as your guide and rudder. The Holy Spirit will provide the wind for your sails.

As the prophet Joel stated:

> And it shall come to pass afterward that I will pour out My Spirit on all flesh; your sons and your daughters shall prophesy, *your old men shall dream dreams, your young men shall see visions.* And also on My menservants and on My maidservants I will pour out My Spirit in those days ... (Joel 2:28, 29).

To all in Christ, I encourage you to be filled with the Spirit, seek His gifts, and above all bear fruit of the Spirit.

> Now may the God of peace who brought up our Lord Jesus from the dead, that great Shepherd of the sheep, through the blood of the everlasting covenant, make you complete in every good work to do His will, working in you what is well pleasing in His sight, through Jesus Christ, to whom be glory forever and ever. Amen (Heb. 13:20–21).

The End

Genesis 1: The Design and Plan for the Kingdom of Heaven,
previously published by Westbow Press

This book, based on exegetical theology, intends to present a unique, theologically sound interpretation of each of the seven days of Creation, which will in turn lead to a much greater, in-depth understanding of the Holy Scriptures—an understanding that will provide a refreshing wind to the churches. The book will engage readers in a spiritual archaeological digging, showing how the first five days of Creation relate to the design and plan for the kingdom of heaven, how the sixth day refers to the implementation of the kingdom, and how the seventh day reveals the handing of the kingdom to the Father. This concept is the unveiling of a mystery that has been either hidden or lost since the Scriptures were written. Knowing this vital information, the reader can embrace a depth to the Creation story that will impact his or her understanding of God and the future He has planned for His creation.

CPSIA information can be obtained at www.ICGtesting.com
Printed in the USA
BVOW031749301011
274797BV00001B/4/P